Civil Liberties and Civil Rights

DAVID C. BAUM
1934-1973

DAVID C. BAUM MEMORIAL LECTURES

Civil Liberties and Civil Rights

Edited and with an Introduction by
VICTOR J. STONE

UNIVERSITY OF ILLINOIS PRESS
Urbana   Chicago   London

Freund, Hastie, and Allen lectures reprinted from the University of Illinois *Law Forum*, volume 1975, number 4. Black and Edwards lectures reprinted from the University of Illinois *Law Forum*, volume 1976, number 2.

Library of Congress Cataloging in Publication Data

Main entry under title:

Civil liberties and civil rights.

(David C. Baum memorial lectures)
"Includes the lectures delivered in 1974-75 and 1975-76."
1.   Civil rights—United States—Addresses, essays,
lectures. I. Stone, Victor J., 1921-   II. Series:
The David C. Baum memorial lectures on civil liberties
and civil rights.
KF4749.A2C49   342'.73'085   77-9428
ISBN 0-252-00620-8

Contents

Introduction

It is melancholic in the extreme that an invaluable commentary on central constitutional issues of our time was generated by a tragic loss to the world of law and legal education. The circumstances are related in the annual announcements of the David C. Baum Memorial Lectures on Civil Liberties and Civil Rights:

The family and friends of David C. Baum have endowed the David C. Baum Memorial Lectures on Civil Liberties and Civil Rights not only in his memory but at his request. Deep concern for the dignity and rights of all men was central to Professor Baum's character and activities.

After receiving his undergraduate and legal education at Harvard University, Professor Baum served as law clerk for Justice Walter V. Schaefer of the Illinois Supreme Court, 1959-60. He then practiced law with the Chicago firm of Ross, McGowan, Hardies and O'Keefe until he joined the faculty of the University of Illinois College of Law in 1963.

Professor Baum was an inspiration to his students and colleagues not only because of the excellence of his teaching, scholarship and public service, but because of his remarkable human qualities. Conscientious and judicious, blending passion for justice with dispassionate objectivity, he inspired the highest level of discourse and endeavor in all who had the privilege of knowing and working with him.

It is hoped that the David C. Baum Memorial Lectures on Civil Liberties and Civil Rights will constitute a fitting memorial to a man whose unrelenting intellectual vigor and moral commitment made his presence in the world of law invaluable.

Professor Baum died early in 1973. The first memorial lecture, on "The Supreme Court's Case Load: Civil Rights and Other Problems," was delivered shortly thereafter by Dean Erwin N. Griswold, who was then Visiting George A. Miller Professor at the University of Illinois College of Law. That lecture was published in the University of Illinois *Law Forum* and later reprinted in booklet form. This volume includes the lectures delivered in 1974-75 and 1975-76.

The lectures given by Professor Freund, Judge Hastie, and Dean Allen in 1974-75 centered upon the impact of the Warren Court on civil liberties and civil rights and upon the immediate sequels to that prodigious era. There could be no more appropriate focus for a series of lectures on civil liberties and civil rights than Chief Justice Warren and the Warren Court. The judicial output of the sixteen Warren years bore significant distinction from that which preceded and from that which followed, and that distinction lay largely in the areas of civil liberties and civil rights.

The Supreme Court of the 1950s and the 1960s is praised and damned and studied as "The Warren Court." Earl Warren gave his name to an era in the life of an enduring institution. Not every chief justice is so recognized. The usage is even more remarkable when one notes that the Court decides by majority vote and that its membership changes with some frequency. Earl Warren came to symbolize the work of the Court over which he presided in large measure because its most notable decisions were recognized to be in substantial measure the consequence of his moral influence. He was a caring man. He cared for those whom he met, for counsel who appeared before the Court, and above all for the oft-times invisible parties in the cases which the Court reviewed. Critics say he cared unwisely and too well, and such judgments have support in cogent argument. The chief justice whose first and last question was "Is it fair?," and for whom legal doctrines were instruments for achieving justice for parties to lawsuits, inspired in many a confidence and devotion that was equaled only by the despair and derision of those who found his directness simplistic and his activism an intrusion on the powers vested by the Constitution in other branches of government.

In eulogizing Earl Warren, one prominent observer of the Court and its personnel wrote: ". . . he applied to the administration of the law his own innate commitments to decency, fairness, equality, integrity and honesty. . . . he forged from those qualities a simple but effective formula for judicial leadership. By giving undiluted devotion to those basic human virtues, in both his personal and his judicial pursuits, he made his chief justiceship an influential fount of equity. He was, in short, the 'chief chancellor of the United States.' No other Chief Justice has ever laid so firm a claim to that title."

Whatever may prove to have been the historic contributions of Chief Justice Warren to adjustments in the balances between state and nation, and among the branches of the federal government—and consensus may be a long time in coming—the spectacle of an honest, vigorous, humane man using the powers of his office to do justice will remain an ennobling spectacle.

Professor Freund's lecture addresses directly and globally the impact on civil liberties and civil rights of the Warren Court's decisions and judicial techniques. Acknowledgment of its achievements is accompanied by identification of flaws in reasoning and of the risks inhering in the judicial use of polemic rhetoric.

Judge Hastie's lecture was delivered less than thirteen months before death terminated his distinguished career. The reconciliation of "affirmative action" with repugnance for racial or ethnic discrimination has become a persistent, divisive issue to which neither courts nor political or ethical leaders have yet furnished untroubling solutions. Judge Hastie's treatment of that thorny problem exemplifies his judicial and scholarly career: a bold, relentless analysis of an area, of its recognized problems, and of the problems implied by proposed solutions; and a synthesis of fact and theory into a just solution that is theoretically extendable into adjacent areas.

Dean Allen reminds us of the backdrop before which the Warren Court played its role in developing specific protections for defendants in criminal cases out of the admonitions of the Bill of Rights and the Fourteenth Amendment. The gaps between rationales, decisions, and prescriptions in the leading criminal law cases challenge both the admirers and the critics of the judicial expansionism of the Warren Court to define and redefine the judicial role in making fundamental social choices. The demands of law enforcers that they be allowed to operate "effectively" to protect the public and the claims of civil libertarians that fair play for the relatively defenseless defendant requires curbs upon effective police and prosecutorial tactics compete daily in judicial and legislative forums, and in the court of public opinion. Dean Allen's profound study of the arguments and the decisions is a primer for enlightened consideration and decision.

The Baum Memorial Lectures for 1975-76 focused more narrowly upon a special aspect of Judge Hastie's lecture on affirmative action. When opportunities are expanding, affirmative action presents problems of allocating surpluses or increases; when economic opportunities are diminishing or contracting, the implications of "affirmative" action ineluctably may be "negative" action against individually faultless persons.

After distinguishing individual responsibility from shared or social responsibility, and both concepts from that of individual guilt, Professor Black calls for affirmative action to right monumental historic wrongs, but only up to the point where a moral dilemma offers only two wrongs as choices. The discrete capacities and incapacities of separate organs of government are highlighted by Professor Black's statement of the judicial dilemma: courts can only choose between adversaries, and in some situations neither should lose. Legislatures, on the other hand, can attempt and finance more comprehensive approaches, spreading costs across society, so that remedying an injustice to one individual need not impose punitive impact on another who does not merit individual punishment.

Professor Edwards brings his vast knowledge of the workings of the labor market to bear upon discrimination in employment. He offers overwhelming historical and statistical evidence of unequal opportunity. What to do? Professor Edwards contends forcefully that notions of fairness must be tailored to specific problems and situations. He argues that however strong our attachment to "neutral principles" as general determinants of judicial decisions, some partisan policies must be employed to some degree to effect salutary change in the ways that employment, retention, and promotion decisions are made in a relatively free labor market in a pluralistic society. There follows exhaustive analysis of the manifestations of discrimination in times of economic stress and of the remedies which have been proposed and attempted. The ultimate question of social morality which Professor Black poses is phrased in its full detail and complexity: Who should pay the cost of remedying the wrongs suffered by the victims of illegal employment discrimination?

Thus were the David C. Baum Memorial Lectures on Civil Liberties and Civil Rights launched at the University of Illinois College of Law. It is our hope that David, who "blend[ed] passion for justice with dispassionate objectivity," would have considered these lectures a fitting memorial.

VICTOR J. STONE

Lecturers

PAUL A. FREUND is Carl M. Loeb Professor, Harvard University Law School, and the author of *On Law and Justice* and *The Supreme Court of the United States*.

WILLIAM H. HASTIE was Senior Circuit Judge, Third Circuit, U.S. Court of Appeals, from 1949 until his death in 1976.

FRANCIS A. ALLEN is Edson R. Sunderland Professor of Law at the University of Michigan. He is the author of *The Borderland of Criminal Justice: Essays in Law and Criminology* and *The Crimes of Politics: Political Dimensions of Criminal Justice*.

CHARLES L. BLACK, JR., is Sterling Professor of Law at Yale University. Among his books are *Impeachment: A Handbook* and *Capital Punishment: The Inevitability of Caprice and Mistake*.

HARRY T. EDWARDS is professor, Harvard University Law School. He has published numerous journal articles.

I. The Supreme Court and Civil Liberties

The Judicial Process in Civil Liberties Cases

PAUL A. FREUND

This lecture can essay only a synoptic view of the Warren Court's treatment of civil liberties and civil rights. The Court, functioning at the outset in the national climate of McCarthyism, endeavored to liberate us from our fears and to recall us to our historic vision of an open and courageous society. In so doing the Court enhanced not only the law, but ourselves as well. Especially to the younger generation, the Court gave hope that our national ideals of freedom and brotherhood might still be redeemed.

Of course the law, and more particularly the judiciary, cannot alone secure a humane society. The business of the law is justice, and though that great end is an inherent expectation of humanity, it is not the only ideal of society, and it is by no means achieved by law alone. In the 18th century Alexander Pope could write: "Of all those ills that mortal men endure/How few are those the law can cause or cure." Although law assumes a larger role in the 20th century, Pope's observation remains pertinent. Consider the great issues of our time: war and peace, poverty and plenty, consumption and conservation of resources, ignorance and education, fear and security in our crowded cities. The law, and particularly judge-made law, can have only a limited impact on these issues. Even in the field of civil liberties and civil rights the impact is fragmentary and may be oblique. The law can give us freedom from governmental censorship of the press, but the quality of the press, its contribution to our understanding and our will, lies in larger measure with the press itself. Thus, responsibility rather than freedom of the press becomes the problematic factor. The same is true of those immensely powerful media, television and motion pictures.

Indeed, a case can be made that the fascination of following the Supreme Court, with all its drama of personalities and clashing opinions, is diversionary in effect, taking our attention away from the pervasive problems and presuppositions of the social system itself. The niceties of criminal procedure are not only fascinating but vital, and yet what of the conditions, psychological and environmental, that breed criminal behavior? What of the concept of punishment itself, its aims and its effectiveness, and what especially of the routine resort to imprisonment, or resort to it in the discretion of a man wearing a robe? One English commentator observed that

[a]n English trial, properly conducted, is one of the best products of our law, provided you walk out of the court before the sentence is given; if you stay to the end, you may find that it takes far less time and enquiry to settle a man's prospects in life than it has taken to find out whether he took a suitcase out of a parked motor car.[1]

The phenomenon is surely not a uniquely British one.

Having said these things by way of introduction, I turn to an examination of the main theme of the Warren Court's contribution. I have suggested that the Court gave us a renewed faith in the traditional ideal of an open society. If I had to choose a one-word characterization, I should say that the major theme of the Court's work and the major constitutional value it strengthened is participation. By this I mean participation both in the horizontal sense of sharing and the vertical sense of freedom from domination. The great risk of liberalism, the reason in some quarters for pronouncing its doom, is that in the guise of legality and open competition a society ends in stratification, in dominance and subservience, like a feudal or oligarchic system. In a liberal state, however, the victims are deluded into fighting for their own subservience under the illusion that their goal is freedom and brotherhood. Unless the professed goals are more nearly matched by reality, the result may be cynicism or moral numbness. Consequently, no more basic contribution could be made to the achievement of a liberal society than to mitigate exclusiveness and domination of power and to promote sharing and shielding. This is an authentic American ideal because it rests on the Constitution as a social compact to which "we, the people" are the subscribers, enjoying mutual rights and owing reciprocal duties.

A court, for all its limitations, can do at least two things to the end of promoting greater participation by the members of the compact. A court can set a tone by articulating the philosophical and legal basis of our community, and it can provide a framework of structure and process that will facilitate, and not obstruct, the forces making for shared powers and responsibilities. Thus, a second word that encompasses the work of the Warren Court and complements participation is "framework."

---

1. R. JACKSON, THE MACHINERY OF JUSTICE IN ENGLAND 184 (1940). Professor Jackson has since become less critical of the sentencing process. *See id.* at 283-314 (6th ed. 1972).

A synoptic view of the signficant decisions of the Warren Court could be a mere inventory of constitutional cases. What is needed is a unifying theme, an organizing principle. The unifying theme we have suggested was the Court's strengthening of a framework for participation. This unity may be illustrated by a brief review of the record in four seemingly diverse fields: suffrage, the first amendment, equal protection, and administration of the criminal law.

The most obvious development was the widening of an effective suffrage. Within this field the most fundamental move was of course reapportionment, enforced in the name of equal protection of the laws, and in the case of the national House of Representatives, enforced somewhat dubiously in the name of the constitutional provision that members of the House be elected by the people.[2] Chief Justice Warren said[3] of the reapportionment cases that if they had been decided earlier, we would not have needed *Brown v. Board of Education*.[4] The claim seems a bit exaggerated, given the effect of reapportionment in increasing the representation of the suburbs, and given indeed the recalcitrance even of urban areas in carrying out their legal obligations to substitute a unitary school system for an officially segregated one. Nevertheless, Warren's comment points up the centrality of fair representation in the process of political responsiveness. The Court's concern with suffrage was also reflected in its striking down the poll tax and outlawing literacy tests under the fifteenth amendment.[5]

The category of cases on the suffrage should also include the decisions vindicating the claims of Adam Clayton Powell and Julian Bond to their elected legislative seats, although the doctrinal bases for these holdings did not rest on the guarantees of voting rights.[6] In effect, the decisions confirmed the right of a district's electors to choose their representative free of a veto by the representative's colleagues. Both the horizontal sharing and freedom from hierarchical domination were at stake in these cases.

The Court's decisions invoking the first amendment are just as vital to participation, since it is by virtue of speech and assembly that the winds of doctrine blow and the freshets of change can course. In *N.Y. Times Co. v. Sullivan*[7] there was a collision, the Court found, between two darlings of the law—the freedom of the press and the interest of an individual in not having his reputation damaged by falsehood. Actually the plaintiff was unable to produce clear and convincing evidence that

---

2. Wesberry v. Sanders, 376 U.S. 1 (1964); Baker v. Carr, 369 U.S. 186 (1962).
3. Ely, *The Chief*, 88 HARV. L. REV. 11, 12 (1974).
4. 347 U.S. 483 (1954).
5. Katzenbach v. Morgan, 384 U.S. 641 (1966); Harper v. Virginia Board of Elections, 383 U.S. 663 (1966); South Carolina v. Katzenbach, 383 U.S. 301 (1966).
6. Powell v. McCormack, 395 U.S. 486 (1969); Bond v. Floyd, 385 U.S. 116 (1966).
7. 376 U.S. 254 (1964).

the paid political advertisement that contained some inaccuracies was directed against him much less that he had suffered any damage to his reputation. Still, the Alabama court sustained a verdict in the plaintiff's favor of half a million dollars. The judgment cried out for reversal, and the Court responded by taking very broad ground indeed. A publisher is not liable unless he published with knowledge of the falsity or with reckless disregard of the truth, if the victim is a public officer or, by extension, a candidate for public office or a public figure. Participation is thus assured to paranoid speakers or publishers whose lies may wound, so long as their paranoia is sincere and their targets are in the public domain.

Freedom of association, too, was given broad shelter. In *United States v. Robel*[8] the Court held that a member of the Communist Party cannot be excluded from employment in a defense plant unless, perhaps, he believed in the illegal purposes of the Party, his employment was in a sensitive position, and the governing statute or regulation was narrowly drawn in these terms. Chief Justice Warren expressed his constitutional faith in these touchingly simple terms:

> Implicit in the term "national defense" is the notion of defending those values and ideals which set this Nation apart. For almost two centuries, our country has taken singular pride in the democratic ideals enshrined in its Constitution, and the most cherished of those ideals have found expression in the First Amendment. It would indeed be ironic if, in the name of national defense, we would sanction the subversion of one of those liberties—the freedom of association—which makes the defense of the Nation worthwhile.[9]

The equal protection guarantee as well has served to provide wider participation in our common life. In the areas of public education, public employment, contract rights, property rights, and inheritance, ancient stereotypes, whether of sexes,[10] or of illegitimates,[11] or of ethnic groups,[12] have given way to at least a prima facie case, if not indeed an irrebuttable premise, of equality under law. How far the public authorities must go, or may go, in righting past wrongs through reverse discrimination raises profound questions of corrective and distributive justice. Although these questions are beyond the scope of this lecture,[13] it may be suggested that the maxim "what's sauce for the goose is sauce

---

8.   389 U.S. 258 (1967).
9.   *Id.* at 264
10.   *See, e.g.*, Weinberger v. Wiesenfeld, 95 S. Ct. 1225 (1975); Frontiero v. Richardson, 411 U.S. 677 (1973).
11.   *E.g.*, Weber v. Aetna Cas. & Sur. Co., 406 U.S. 164 (1972); Glona v. American Guarantee & Liab. Ins. Co., 391 U.S. 73 (1968); Levy v. Louisiana, 391 U.S. 68 (1968).
12.   *See, e.g.*, Brown v. Board of Educ., 347 U.S. 483 (1954); Hernandez v. Texas, 347 U.S. 475 (1954).
13.   Reverse discrimination is the subject of a separate lecture by Judge Hastie . *See* Hastie, *Affirmative Action in Vindicating Civil Rights*, 1975 U. ILL. L.F. 502; reprinted on p. 13 of this volume.

for the gander" is less than a self-evident truth. Surely it is not true if the sauce is estrogen, and it may not be true if goose and gander were given highly disparate diets in the past.

Finally, this inventory must also include the administration of criminal law. Although the issue of participation is not as evident in the area of criminal procedure, participation is diminished if the rules, for example, with respect to the assistance of counsel in fact operate on a discriminatory basis against the poor or the ignorant. Furthermore, this class of cases more generally raises the issue of participation in the sense of freedom from domination. The right to counsel in all serious criminal cases, the right to a jury trial in contempt proceedings of a certain gravity, the safeguards required for confessions and for indentification at police lineups, and the mandatory exclusion of illegally obtained evidence are all phases of an enlarged participation in one or a double sense.

The Warren Court's record in these areas is remarkably impressive. Questioning it in certain details may seem as ungracious as examining the Statue of Liberty as a work of sculpture. Questions have been raised, however, and academics in particular have a professional license to judge the judges. Justice Holmes used to say that he did not mind when the law reviews criticized him: "It is when the lads say 'Mr. Justice Holmes was correct' that I find them insufferable." Today judges can hardly complain of an excess of this kind of suffering.

One question that has been asked is whether the Warren Court, in its freely exercised judicial vetoes, was in truth simply another Taft Court, but of the left. If the suggested unifying theme of the Warren Court is correct, the comparison is unfair because a concern with the framework of participation, with structure and process, is a judicial function far more legitimate than the Taft Court's disagreement with the legislative outcomes of that process, whether they be minimum-wage or price-control or child-labor laws.

A more troublesome issue is whether the Court's major decisions were too absolute in nature. The decisions were absolute in the sense that they characteristically mandated one and only one means of complying with a constitutional guarantee that does not itself prescribe a particular solution or sanction to satisfy the guarantee. If the Court decides that a state law or practice cannot be squared with the Constitution, the question remains whether the Court will indicate a range of valid solutions or will specify an exclusive means to satisfy the constitutional objective. I became sensitive to this judicial choice when serving as law clerk to Justice Brandeis. The first case on which I worked had reached the stage of a final draft of the Justice's opinion. Feeling the surge of power that wells up in a law clerk, I wrote out with a flourish what was designed as the final, resounding sentence of the opinion: "Accordingly the judgment is reversed and the cause remanded to the

Supreme Court of Idaho for further proceedings in conformity with this opinion." Even this contribution, however, was wrong. "That is the form we use in reversing and remanding to a federal court," the Justice said. "When we remand to a state court we say 'for further proceedings not inconsistent with this opinion.' " His point, perhaps, was a small one, and yet not unimportant even as a matter of diplomatic protocol. If the difference is more than formal, and if it determines whether a state does or does not retain some latitutde in devising alternative legislative measures, it raises the question whether the Court has moved from a judicial judgment that a law is invalid to a legislative judgment in mandating a specific kind of replacement.

Legislative malapportionment, in the sense of districts arbitrarily disparate in population, called for correction in the name of equal protection or the guarantee of a republican form of government. What is less clear is that in rectifying malapportionment the sole permissible criterion must be equality of numbers to the virtual exclusion of such factors as political boundaries of local units, geographic and economic peculiarities, political configurations, and the philosophy underlying a bicameral legislature. A ruling that substantial equality of population must be the prima facie goal but that still allows consideration of these other factors would have recognized both the arbitrariness of many existing apportionments and the latitude of judgment concerning the fairness of various schemes of representation.[14]

Similarly, in the field of political libel, a judgment of half a million dollars against a newspaper for a paid civil rights advertisement that contained some inaccuracies but did not refer to the plaintiff and that could scarcely have harmed his reputation called for reversal if freedom of the press was to have real meaning. Less clear is the Court's adoption of a single standard of liability for the defamation of a public officer or public figure. The standard requires proof that the statement was published with knowledge of its falsity or with reckless disregard of its truth or falsity. A combination of other factors might have struck an equally permissible balance between reputation and robust political expression. The Court, for example, might have approved a standard of due care on the part of the publisher, coupled with a requirement of actual damages to the victim as a limit on recovery.[15]

---

14. More recently, where state legislative reapportionment is at issue, the Court has interpreted the decisions of the Warren Court to allow consideration of these other factors and to bar judicial veto of relatively minor and nondiscriminatory deviations from the ideal of one person, one vote. *See, e.g.,* White v. Regester, 412 U.S. 755 (1973); Gaffney v. Cummings, 412 U.S. 735 (1973); Mahan v. Howell, 410 U.S. 315 (1973). Contrast with these cases the Court's strict adherence to the ideal required of Congressional districting plans. *See, e.g.,* White v. Weiser, 412 U.S. 783 (1973).

15. *Compare* Gertz v. Robert Welch, Inc., 418 U.S. 323 (1974), where these standards were in fact applied in a case involving a discussion of a public issue, not public officers or public figures.

In the realm of criminal procedure the Court also viewed the constitutional guarantees as requiring a single instrumental rule rather than a range of alternatives. Thus, the Court mandated the exclusionary rule for the fruits of unreasonable searches and seizures in state courts,[16] although a discretionary rule, if coupled with a right of action for liquidated damages against the state, may commend itself to responsible lawmakers as a preferable accommodation between the search for truth and an effective deterrent to unlawful conduct by the police. This alternative would have the advantage of publicizing those illegal searches and seizures that do not turn up evidence or for other reasons do not eventuate in criminal trials. Thus, the aggregate deterrent effect, so far as it rests on public attitudes, could be expected to be greater than under a mandatory rule excluding reliable evidence.

The requirement that counsel be offered to a suspect during a lineup for identification[17] was a response to a glaringly unfair practice. And yet a remedy that places counsel in the role of a witness is not an ideal solution. The requirement might have been ordained in those cases in which a state has not chosen to employ some equally effective means of assuring fairness, such as videotaping the lineup-identification process. In the confession cases the Court did indeed advert to the possibility of some alternative, equally effective, to the *Miranda* warnings.[18] The warnings, however, were spelled out with such emphasis and particularity, and alternatives were mentioned with such generality, that the option of a different safeguard for the voluntariness of a confession was left obscured.

If we ask why the Court has taken an absolutist approach, the answer probably lies in a distrust of the discretion of other courts and of lawmaking bodies, an apprehension of evasion, or the prospect of continuous scrutiny by the Court of dubiously marginal measures to determine whether they are "not inconsistent with" federal guarantees. The same understandable impulse moved Justice Black to formulate the "incorporation theory" of the fourteenth amendment, giving it a meaning no less and no more inclusive than the specific guarantees of the Bill of Rights. The difficulties with that theory, even in hands as resourceful as Justice Black's, are too familiar to be recounted at length. Absoluteness would be purchased at the cost of including in the due process guarantee against the states a specific federal mandate of a jury trial in all common law actions involving more than twenty dollars and leaving in limbo some basic assurances that happen to be placed in the body of the Constitution rather than in the Bill of Rights, most notably the guarantee of jury trial in criminal cases. What was said of the Rule in

---

16. Mapp v. Ohio, 367 U.S. 643 (1961).
17. United States v. Wade, 388 U.S. 218 (1967).
18. Miranda v. Arizona, 384 U.S. 436, 467 (1966).

Shelley's Case[19] can be said as well of the fourteenth amendment: you can put it in a nutshell, but can you keep it there?

In addition to questions about imposing absolute or exclusive sanctions to achieve constitutional ends, another troublesome issue is whether some of the Warren Court's major decisions were too uncertain in their rationale. The query is not a pedantic one, for theories have consequences, for good or ill. In the reapportionment problem a central issue concerns the nature of the voters' grievance. Is it that each voter has been denied a right to a proportionate share in the choice of his representative equal to that of a voter in another district in the choice of the latter's representative? Or is the complaint that the voters in a district, as a polity, are entitled to fair representation in the legislative assembly? The former view permits no latitude for factors other than arithmetic comparisons. At the same time, it allows less room for the review of abuses in districting not involving numerical disparities, such as political gerrymandering that satisfies the constraints of equal population.

In *Brown v. Board of Education*,[20] the key statement is that "separate educational facilities are inherently unequal." The term "inherently" in this context can mean one of two things. It can mean that such facilities are upon investigation empirically unequal, as when we say that men and women are inherently unequal in muscular strength. The inclusion of the celebrated footnote eleven in the opinion suggests the empirical view. The term "inherently" may mean, however, that separate facilities are unequal by definition within the meaning of equal protection of the laws. Under this interpretation, making access to a given public facility depend on color is a denial of equal protection without regard to sociological or psychological evidence, as when we say "six of one are equal to half a dozen of the other." What is wanted is not a disquisition on the Kantian distinction between statements that are true synthetically and those that are true analytically. Rather, all that is wanted is sensitivity to the different implications that are to be drawn from the two meanings, because if the proposition about separate facilities is based on observation and investigation, then there is an implicit invitation continually to reexamine the proposition in light of further studies.

The basis of the exclusionary rule for illegally obtained evidence likewise has been left ambiguous. It may be simply a deterrent to police misconduct, as suggested by the Court's decision not to make the rule retroactive to cases in which the conduct has already occurred. Under this rationale there would be room for experimentation with alternative

---

19. *See* Van Grutten v. Foxwell, [1897] A.C. 658, 671 (Lord McNaghten), *quoted in* Leach, *Perpetuities in a Nutshell*, 51 Harv. L. Rev. 638 n. (1938).
20. 347 U.S. 483, 495 (1954).

deterrents. On the other hand, the rule may be based largely on a judgment that the admission of evidence tainted in its procurement would be a blot on the integrity of the judicial process itself. Under this view there is no reason for the prevailing requirement of "standing" to object to the evidence;[21] any defendant should be entitled to raise the objection, not merely one who has a proprietary or possessory interest in the premises searched or the material seized.

More important, however, than a negative critique would be an effort to construct alternative solutions and test their effectiveness and validity. One limitation on courts as designers of correctives is that they naturally incline toward measures that can be taken on the operating level by judges and lawyers. Measures that may require a different form of machinery, especially if substantial outlays would be required, are likely to be a last recourse for appellate courts, whereas they may properly be a first resort for legislatures. It would be a lamentable result of the seeming absoluteness of instrumental decisions if they produced a stifling of the inventive legislative impulse, or if the energies of lawmakers were exhausted in equally absolute denunciation.

It should be remembered that the Court over which John Marshall presided was given to absoluteness of statement: the power of Congress over interstate commerce is exclusive; the power to tax involves the power to destroy; grants by the state cannot be altered without violating the obligation of contract guarantee. These doctrines bedevilled the law until some counterweights were subsequently recognized. And yet Marshall's achievement survives these exuberances. Justice Holmes reminded his generation:

> When we celebrate Marshall we celebrate at the same time and indivisibly the inevitable fact that the oneness of the nation and the supremacy of the national Constitution were declared to govern the dealings of man with man by the judgments and decrees of the most august of courts.[22]

The oneness of the nation, physically and economically, was fostered by the Marshall Court. The great theme of the Warren Court is the oneness of the nation in its democratic vistas. Neither vision is commanded by the Constitution; both are faithful to it. Not without reason is the eagle our national symbol. As an emblem for constitutional judges I would only add to the soaring vision of the eagle the prudential scrutiny of the owl.

---

21. *See* Alderman v. United States, 394 U.S. 165 (1969).
22. THE OCCASIONAL SPEECHES OF JUSTICE OLIVER WENDELL HOLMES 133 (M. Howe ed. 1962).

Affirmative Action in Vindicating Civil Rights

WILLIAM H. HASTIE

On a single day in April, 1971, the Supreme Court handed down several decisions concerning racially segregated public education. These cases provide an instructive starting point for a discussion of the congeries of legal situations and problems connected with racial discrimination that have come to be subsumed under the heading "affirmative action." Ever since the epochal 1954 and 1955 decisions in *Brown v. Board of Education*,[1] it had been apparent that a trial court, exercising the traditional function and power of a court of equity, may and often should specify steps that the public authorities must take to remedy their unconstitutionally imposed system of racially segregated schools.[2] The 1971 cases are noteworthy for the Supreme Court's discussions of and rulings upon particular schemes of remedial affirmative action.

Each of these cases arose in a state that had required and maintained separate schools for white and black children in 1954 when the Supreme Court invalidated that system as inconsistent with the equal protection clause of the fourteenth amendment. Each state had abandoned the formal requirement of racial segregation and substantial numbers of white and black children were attending school together in the school district that was before the court. Questions persisted, however, regarding how far public school authorities should go and what affirmative action they might take, or should be required to take, to fulfill their obligation to desegregate their schools.

One case[3] arose in Mobile, Alabama, where a major highway bisected the metropolitan area. The school board had inaugurated a desegregation plan under which it divided the city into two school attendance zones with the major highway serving as their dividing line. The board then assigned children living within each attendance zone to

---

1. 349 U.S. 294 (1955); 347 U.S. 483 (1954).
2. The second *Brown* opinion directed the district courts in that and companion cases to retain jurisdiction during a "period of transition" to consider proposed desegregation plans and, "guided by equitable principles," to enter appropriate orders and decrees. 349 U.S. at 300.
3. Davis v. School Comm'rs, 402 U.S. 33 (1971).

particular schools in that zone. Through this process each zone's schools were as fairly and effectively integrated as that zone's racial population pattern would permit. However, more than 90 percent of the black children lived on the same side of the highway. Consequently, under the board's plan the schools in one zone were predominately black whereas in the other zone they were overwhelmingly white, even though each zone, considered separately, was integrated as completely as possible.

Chief Justice Burger, speaking for the unanimous Court from which Chief Justice Warren had recently retired, recognized the intrinsic merits of "unified geographic zones" that were designed to facilitate neighborhood school attendance and to avoid the necessity of children crossing a major highway. Nevertheless, he concluded that the pursuit of this legitimate objective did not excuse the failure of the school authorities to fashion an affirmative desegregation plan that would "achieve the greatest possible degree of . . . desegregation, taking into account the practicalities of the situation."[4] He added, "The measure of any desegregation plan is its effectiveness."[5]

An earlier case[6] arose in Montgomery, Alabama. There a district court found that for more than a year the local school board had made no substantial progress in carrying out the court's order to desegregate the faculties of the formerly separate white and black schools. The court ordered the school district to assign teachers of the other race to each school that formerly had a faculty of all of the same race in proportion not less than one to five. The order applied to the ensuing year and was subject to future orders for subsequent years. The Supreme Court approved this requirement of interim racial faculty quotas and thus rejected the often stated generalization that government itself must always be "color blind" in the sense of avoiding different treatment of racially defined groups of people.

Two other cases in the 1971 group deal more directly with the notion of color blindness. In *McDaniel v. Barresi*[7] the Court reversed a decision of the Georgia Supreme Court that had enjoined implementation of a county's school desegregation plan. The state court held that the plan violated the equal protection clause "by treating students differently because of their race."[8] The county redrew its attendance zones so that black students would be more widely dispersed, with the objective that blacks would constitute about one-third of the enrollment in most of the county's schools. Moreover, the plan assigned students living in certain small black residential enclaves to predominantly white schools outside of what geographically would have been their attendance zone.

---

4. *Id.* at 37.
5. *Id.*
6. United States v. Montgomery Bd. of Educ., 395 U.S. 225 (1969).
7. 402 U.S. 39 (1971).
8. Barresi v. Browne, 226 Ga. 456, 459, 175 S.E.2d 649, 652 (1970).

Holding that this plan was valid, the Chief Justice, writing for the Court, first repeated the metaphorical statement of an earlier case that it was the constitutional duty of those who had maintained separate racial schools to eliminate racial discrimination "root and branch."[9] He then explicitly recognized that

This remedial process . . . will almost invariably require that students be assigned differently because of their race. . . . Any other approach would freeze the status quo that is the very target of the desegregation process.[10]

On the same day the Court dealt with an enactment of the North Carolina legislature that had employed the concept that the Constitution is color blind to prohibit the inclusion of certain features in desegregation plans. The statute forbade the assignment of any student to any school "on account of race . . . or for the purpose of creating a balance or ratio of race . . . ."[11] It also prohibited involuntary busing of students.[12]

The Court, again speaking through the new Chief Justice, recognized that the North Carolina statute "exploits an apparently neutral form of control . . . by directing that . . . [school assignment plans] be 'color blind' . . . ."[13] The Chief Justice rejected this device, observing that "[j]ust as the race of students must be considered in determining whether a constitutional violation has occurred, so also must race be considered in formulating a remedy."[14] He reasoned that the school authorites must have at their disposal "all reasonable methods . . . to formulate an effective remedy." Then, more specifically, he added that interim racial ratios, alone or implemented by bussing, might be reasonable methods in particular situations and that, therefore, the state could not outlaw them.[15]

The extent of the Court's commitment to whatever remedies may be reasonable and practical to redress the constitutional inequality inherent in segregated public schools is summed up in yet another of the April, 1971, cases: "The remedy . . . may be administratively awkward, inconvenient, and even bizarre in some situations and may impose burdens on some; but . . . [that] cannot be avoided in the interim period. . . ."[16] That language gains force from the fact that the Court used it in approving a far-reaching, judicially-imposed desegregation

---

9. McDaniel v. Barresi, 402 U.S. 39, 41 (1971), *quoting* Green v. County School Bd., 391 U.S. 430, 437-38 (1968).
10. *Id. Compare* Chief Judge Coffin's observation in Associated Gen. Contractors, Inc. v. Altshuler, 490 F.2d 9, 16 (1st Cir. 1973), "[o]ur society cannot be completely color blind in the short term if we are to have a color blind society in the long term."
11. N.C. Gen. Stat. §§ 115-176.1 (1975).
12. *Id.*
13. Board of Educ. v. Swann, 402 U.S. 43, 46 (1971).
14. *Id.* at 45.
15. *Id.* at 46.
16. Swann v. Charlotte-Mecklenburg Bd. of Educ., 402 U.S. 1, 28 (1971).

plan for Charlotte-Mecklenburg, a North Carolina school district that included the City of Charlotte and its surrounding suburbs. With blacks concentrated in the center of the city and whites in the outer city and surrounding suburbs, the district court had ordered "that efforts be made to reach a 71-29 ratio [of whites to blacks] in the various schools" throughout the district. To that end the district court designed wedge-shaped attendance zones, each widening out from a small center city portion to include a broad suburban area. The Court deemed imposition of this affirmative action lawful and proper, even though the Court explicitly recognized it as "administratively awkward" and, to some, inconvenient and burdensome.

Individually and collectively these cases indicate that Justice Harlan's often quoted dictum in *Plessy v. Ferguson*[17] that "[o]ur Constitution is color blind" is an overbroad aphorism. In context it seems to have been a rhetorical restatement of the Justice's immediately preceding observation that, although whites in all likelihood will continue to be the dominant racial group in America, "in the view of the Constitution, in the eye of the law. . . . [t]here is no caste here."[18]   Moreover, the dictum has validity when, as in the *Plessy* situation itself, the wrong of exclusion from or segregation in places of public accommodation and resort can be remedied, simply and fully, by disregarding race in the acceptance and accommodation of patrons.[19] In contrast, the institutionalization of racially segregated public education often cannot be corrected fully, as it must be, without affirmative action that takes race into account and, in a transitional period at least, employs race as a determinant of appropriate corrective action that affects whites and blacks differently. In these circumstances today's Supreme Court apparently adheres to the view that an otherwise appropriate remedy subjecting blacks and whites to different treatment by government does not in itself deny members of either group constitutionally required equal protection of the laws. Moreover, the Court has explicitly recognized that in some cases this process will impose burdens on individuals. Examples of these burdens include transfers from schools near students' homes to more distant schools and transfers to schools with inferior equipment or less outstanding teachers. Although all of these disadvantages are proper considerations, they are not, in themselves, decisive against particular remedial attendance plans deemed essential to complete elimination of state-required or state-sanctioned racial segregation.[20]

---

17. 163 U.S. 537, 559 (1896).
18. *Id.*
19. *E.g.*, Johnson v. Virginia, 373 U.S. 61 (1963) (courtroom); Turner v. City of Memphis, 369 U.S. 350 (1962) (restaurant); Gayle v. Browder, 352 U.S. 903 (1956) (mem.).
20. In a different area, see United States v. E.I. duPont de Nemours & Co., 366 U.S. 316 (1961), for a comparable imposition of an extremely costly requirement of stock divestiture as an equitable remedy deemed necessary to achieve complete elimination of a tendency toward monopoly.

A final noteworthy point is that the Court has been careful to say that, beyond what the Constitution requires, public school authorities are free to reorganize school attendance to obtain so-called "racial balance" in enrollment throughout a school system.[21] Because school boards are free to do this on their own initiative, no constitutional impediment exists to state legislative or administrative action that goes beyond constitutional requirements and, as a matter of public policy, directs school boards to make reasonable efforts to cause the racial mix in schools throughout the district to reflect district-wide racial population ratios. A few states have these statutes now,[22] and the state supreme court has sustained the constitutionality of the Illinois statute.[23]

Our next concern is the proper application these concepts and rulings on affirmative action in public education have to other areas in which racial minorities have been and still are disadvantaged. Of particular concern are access to housing and opportunities for initial employment and subsequent promotion. After that we may be in better position to discuss yet another educational problem, the use of racial considerations in individual admissions to colleges and universities. The much-publicized *DeFunis* litigation[24] has recently heightened interest in this latter area.

In a typical public school segregation case a court, acting on the complaint of some aggrieved member or members of a segregated minority, first tries the basic issue of actionable wrongdoing and then, having found an actionable denial of constitutional right in the organization or administration of the school system, undertakes to fashion an appropriate remedial order. Fair employment practice litigation may start and proceed in the same way. In recent years the Supreme Court and the courts of appeals have given a broad reading to the provisions of the 1870 Civil Rights Act that guarantees to "all persons . . . the same right to make and enforce contracts" and the same property rights as those "enjoyed by white citizens."[25] Viewing the exclusion of blacks

---

21. School authorities . . . might well conclude, for example, that in order to prepare students to live in a pluralistic society each school should have a prescribed ratio of Negro to white students reflecting the proportion in the district as a whole. To do this as an educational policy is within the broad discretionary powers of the school authorities . . . .
Swann v. Charlotte-Mecklenburg Bd. of Educ., 402 U.S. 1, 16 (1971). For a summary but useful statement of "Evils of the Racially Imbalanced Schools," see Fiss, *Racial Imbalance in the Public Schools: The Constitutional Concepts*, 78 HARV. L. REV. 564, 567-70 (1965).
22. CAL. ADMINISTRATIVE CODE, tit. v, §§ 2001, 2010-11; ILL. REV. STAT. ch. 122, §§ 10-21.3 (1973); MASS. ANN. LAWS ch. 71, §§ 37C-D (1971).
23. Tometz v. Board of Educ., 39 Ill. 2d 593, 237 N.E.2d 498 (1961). *Compare* Offermann v. Nitkowski, 378 F.2d 22 (2d Cir. 1967), in which a school board acted without statutory mandate.
24. DeFunis v. Odegaard, 82 Wash. 2d 11, 507 P.2d 1169 (1971), *vacated as moot,* 416 U.S. 312 (1974).
25. 42 U.S.C. § 1981 (1970). The seminal decision, Jones v. Mayer Co., 392 U.S. 409 (1968), finds in § 2 of the thirteenth amendment, which authorizes Congress to

from employment opportunity enjoyed by whites as a "badge or incident" of slavery that was outlawed by the thirteenth amendment, the courts have recognized the 1870 Civil Rights Act, and more recently title VII of the 1964 Civil Rights Act, as validly prohibiting private employers and labor unions from denying minorities equal access to job opportunities.[26] Thus, an aggrieved minority worker may now obtain legal redress for private or public employment discrimination in much the same way that aggrieved blacks have for many years been obtaining equitable relief from public school segregation.

In some cases employment discrimination based on race may be more difficult to prove than state-imposed educational segregation. This has led to litigation over the probative value of particular evidence or its effect on the burden of proof.[27] Once the court has validly determined that a particular employer's or union's employment practices are invidiously discriminatory, however, the propriety of specified affirmative corrective requirements may be judged by analogy to the Supreme Court's approval of similar far-reaching and often burdensome impositions on wrongdoing school boards. For example, in the Montgomery, Alabama, school case[28] the Court approved an interim remedial requirement that assigned school teachers throughout the system to achieve specified minimum racial ratios in the faculty of each school. In some other city one may prove that invidious racial discrimination has restricted appointments or promotions of other public employees, such as librarians, policemen, firemen, or hospital personnel. In such a case an interim remedial requirement that mandates the appointment of equal numbers or some other ratio of whites and blacks or their promotion from fairly established lists of eligibles seems as consistent with equity

---

implement the constitutional prohibition of slavery by "appropriate legislation," adequate authority for legislative proscription of private action that in effect continues the involuntary subordination of blacks in our social and economic order.

26. Beudreaux v. Baton Rouge Maritime Contracting Co., 437 F.2d 1011 (5th Cir. 1971); Waters v. Wisconsin Steel Works, 427 F.2d 476, 484 (7th Cir. 1970). By 1971 the Supreme Court seems to have viewed the power of Congress to proscribe private denials of equal employment opportunity as too clear to require discussion. *See* Griggs v. Duke Power Co., 401 U.S. 424 (1971).

27. Controversy often has centered upon the evidentiary significance of a gross disparity between the percentage of blacks employed by the alleged discriminator in some type of work and the percentage of blacks in some other universe, such as the local population, or some labor pool. In most of the cases, the statistically demonstrated disparity has been very great and this alone or combined with other circumstances has served to create a logical inference of racial discrimination. Accordingly, courts have held that a prima facie case of discrimination has been established and that the alleged discriminator must then bear the burden of going forward and persuading the trier of fact that his employment practices have been nondiscriminatory. *E.g.*, Morrow v. Crisler, 491 F.2d 1053 (5th Cir. 1974); United States v. Hayes Int'l Corp., 456 F.2d 112 (5th Cir. 1972); Carter v. Gallagher, 452 F.2d 315 (8th Cir. 1971), *cert. denied*, 406 U.S. 950 (1972); United States v. IBEW Local 38, 428 F.2d 144 (6th Cir. 1970). *See also* the cautionary discussion of this use of racial statistics in Fiss, *A Theory of Fair Employment Law*, 38 U. Chi. L. Rev. 235, 270-74 (1971).

28. United States v. Montgomery Bd. of Educ., 395 U.S. 225 (1969).

and fairness to those whites who may be disadvantaged by the requirement as was the racial ratio imposed in the assignment of Montgomery
school teachers or in reshaping attendance zones in Charlotte-Mecklenburg. Indeed, the propriety of imposing interim remedial racial employment quotas or ratios on wrongdoing employers and labor unions has
been a major issue in federal litigation throughout the country. With
notable uniformity, the courts of appeals have sanctioned these remedial
impositions.[29] Characteristically, the cases have disclosed long-continued
discrimination against minority workers and significant resistance to
change. In these circumstances the courts, taking their cue from the
segregated school cases, have reasoned that the equitable objective of
eliminating obvious, continuing consequences of past invidious discrimination as fully and expeditiously as seems fair and feasible justifies the
interim imposition of some racial formula to control hiring and promotion. The results of 2 decades of "deliberate speed" in correcting segregated education have not commended that pace to today's chancellors,
who are given the judicial responsibility of fashioning adequate remedies
for unfair employment practices.[30]

Somewhat more difficult to analogize to the school cases is the case
of an administrative determination that industry-wide or craft-wide
employment discrimination exists throughout an area and the resulting
administrative imposition of area-wide affirmative action requirements
upon an entire industry without any finding that a particular employer
has been guilty of discriminatory practices. The controversy over the so-
called "Philadelphia Plan" exemplifies this problem. Beginning in 1941
a series of executive orders and recent congressional enactments[31] have
required that employers who accept contractual undertakings for or

---

29. Rios v. Steamfitters Local 638, 501 F.2d 622 (2d Cir. 1974) (union in New
York City required to admit at least 30% nonwhites to each new group accepted for
apprentice training and to achieve 30% nonwhite union membership within four years);
Morrow v. Crisler, 491 F.2d 1053 (5th Cir. 1974) (district court directed to consider
whether temporary requirement of one-to-one or two-to-one racial hiring ratios might be
necessary to accelerate correction of long continued pattern of employment discrimination); Vulcan Soc'y of N.Y. Fire Dep't, Inc. v. Civil Service Comm'n, 490 F.2d 387 (2d
Cir. 1973) (appointment of one eligible member of a minority for every three majority
eligibles until new list of eligibles should be established in a nondiscriminatory way);
Associated Gen. Contractors, Inc. v. Altshuler, 490 F.2d 9 (1st Cir. 1973), *cert. denied*,
416 U.S. 957 (1974) (20% ratio of minority employee man hours to total employee man
hours in each job category in construction projects); United States v. N.L. Indus., Inc.,
479 F.2d 354, 373 (8th Cir. 1973) (promotion of whites and blacks in equal numbers to
foreman is required until 15 of one hundred foremen are black).

30. *See also* United States v. Dothard, 373 F. Supp. 504 (M.D. Ala. 1974), in
which the court's own experience with charges of employment discrimination in Alabama
state agencies had demonstrated that an injunction merely prohibiting such discrimination was ineffective, but that the requirement that a particular agency work toward the
goal of specified numbers of black employees had achieved substantial minority employment.

31. *See* Titles VI and VIII of the Civil Rights Act of 1964, 42 U.S.C. §§ 200d-e
(1970); Exec. Order No. 8,802, 3 C.F.R. 957 (Comp. 1938-43); Exec. Order No.
11,114, 3 C.F.R. 185 (Supp. 1963). *See also* Exec. Order No. 11,246, 3 C.F.R. 418
(1974).

financed by the United States shall not engage in racial or other invidiously discriminatory employment practices. Federal agencies charged with administering these requirements have resorted to various expedients to implement them. The Philadelphia Plan[32] is typical. The plan requires employers who bid for large federally-assisted construction contracts in the Philadelphia area to agree to make a good faith effort to achieve specified minority employment goals. The federal agency establishes and publishes these goals for several building trades in terms of percentages of minority employees the contractor must hire in each craft. For example, in 1971 an acceptable bid had to include the contractor's plan to achieve the employment of minority ironworkers within a range of 11 to 15 percent of his work force in this craft.

In predetermining this and similar goals the administrative agency utilized government and industry studies of the labor force and market and also conducted its own research and analysis. In addition, it held public hearings on the problem of minority employment and the need for and the appropriate kind of remedial action. In this way it determined that the general practice of Philadelphia area contractors was to hire a work force anew for each new large construction project, utilizing the hiring halls of recognized craft unions for recruitment purposes. The agency also found that particular building trade unions excluded or discriminated against black members of the craft, substantial number of whom were available for employment. These racially discriminatory practices of the unions, combined with the contractors' reliance on union hiring halls, reduced the number of minority members of crafts to about 1 percent of the total workmen employed in six major building trades. Finally, the administrative agency found that contractors could adopt and move effectively toward the specified percentage goals for minority hiring in these crafts "without adverse impact on the existing labor force."

Obviously, this administrative imposition of affirmative action requirements differs significantly from a judicial one. The agency action is based on an ex parte administrative determination that employment discrimination against minorities is prevalent throughout a defined area. In contrast, the judicial imposition of similar requirements on an individual employer or union as a remedy for that defendant's unlawful discrimination follows an adjudication conducted in an adversary proceeding. In the latter situation, as in the public education cases, the wrongdoer himself is in no position to complain that it is burdensome to change his unlawful ways. At most he can complain that the remedy is inequitable because it may be unfair to majority workers. However, when an administrative agency decrees that all employers who wish to

---

32. 2 CCH EMPLOYMENT PRACTICE GUIDE §§ 16, 175-76 (1969). For an elaboration of the operation of the plan, see Note, *The Philadelphia Plan: Equal Employment Opportunity in the Construction Trades*, 6 COLUM. J.L. & SOCIAL PROBLEMS 187 (1970). For similar plans in effect in other metropolitan areas, see 41 C.F.R. §§ 60-5 to -11.

bid for government contracts must take certain action, the agency imposes an industry-wide obligation without affording an individual employer the opportunity to show in advance that he is not a wrongdoer and that the affirmative imposition will be unfair to him.

Nevertheless, this method of dealing with problems is not peculiar to the area of present concern. Regulatory agencies characteristically proceed in this manner in formulating and imposing duties on a regulated group.[33] Congress has thus wisely prescribed procedures in the Administrative Procedure Act[34] that these agencies must follow to ensure that those subject to regulation as well as other interested persons have an opportunity to submit information and opinion before the agency acts.[35] Moreover, one who deems himself aggrieved by the application of a general regulation to him may challenge it in court as arbitrary, unreasonable, or improperly promulgated.[36] Much of administrative law is concerned with the principles and concepts developed in the course of such litigation. The point here is merely that administrative determination of the need for and reasonableness of regulatory schemes like the Philadelphia Plan is not essentially different from other agency determinations that we have long since recognized as proper and authoritative. Similarly, these actions are subject to judicial review of their justification and reasonableness. Indeed, the Court of Appeals for the Third Circuit has reviewed the Philadelphia Plan and has found it to be a reasonable regulative scheme, fully justified by circumstances that an administrative agency properly found to exist in the Philadelphia area.[37]

Affirmative action in connection with urban housing discrimination also brings controversial questions of legal right and social justice into sharp focus. Evidence exists, which many responsible persons find compelling and persuasive, that racial residential segregation harms a disadvantaged minority, exacerbates racial tension, and seriously impedes the solution of major urban problems.[38] Accordingly, public agencies and private persons from time to time have undertaken affirmative action to correct or lessen what they reasonably view as a very harmful distortion of community life.[39]

---

33. *See generally* 1 K. Davis, Administrative Law Treatise, chs. 5-7 (1958).
34. 5 U.S.C. §§ 551-59 (1970).
35. *Id.* § 553.
36. *Id.* §§ 701-06 (1970).
37. Contractors Ass'n v. Secretary of Labor, 442 F.2d 159 (3d Cir.), *cert. denied*, 404 U.S. 854 (1971); Comment, *The Philadelphia Plan: A Study in the Dynamics of Creative Power*, 39 U. Chi. L. Rev. 723 (1972). For cases approving various local plans, see Associated Gen. Contractors, Inc. v. Altshuler, 490 F.2d 9 (1st Cir. 1973), *cert. denied*, 416 U.S. 957 (1974); Southern Ill. Builders Ass'n v. Ogilvie, 471 F.2d 680 (7th Cir. 1972); Weiner v. Cuyahoga Community College Dist., 19 Ohio St. 2d 35, 249 N.E.2d 907 (1969), *cert. denied*, 396 U.S. 1004 (1970).
38. C. Abrams, Race Bias in Housing 20-25 (1949); M. Deutsch & M. Collins, Interracial Housing 122 (1950); S. Tenenbaum, Why Men Hate 33 (1947).
39. *See* McGhee & Ginger, *The House I Live In*, 46 Cornell L.Q. 194, 225 (1961).

Large new public or private urban housing developments in multi-racial communities are likely to create racial occupancy issues. Documented experience in urban communities that include substantial non-white minorities shows that a racially integrated residential development is likely to remain integrated as long as, and only as long as, residents anticipate that nonwhites will not constitute more than a minor fraction, apparently about one-third, of the residents.[40] Once minority occupancy increases substantially beyond that, however, the white residents become apprehensive and begin to move elsewhere, with the result that the newly developed area soon becomes a ghetto. Avoiding this result is a major concern of any developer who believes that integrated occupancy is advantageous to both white and nonwhite occupants as well as to the entire urban community. Accordingly, a private developer or a public housing agency may impose racial restrictions, sometimes called "benign quotas," in the acceptance of tenants or purchasers to the extent calculated to create and maintain an integrated community.

Because blacks characteristically experience far greater difficulty than whites in finding decent urban housing, the immediate consequence of this restrictive practice is to deny some black applicants, because of their race, access to housing that they seek and urgently need. Thus, although the objective of the racial restriction is to prevent the establishment of an urban black ghetto and to promote a constructive, integrated residential community, rejected black applicants may believe and charge that the developer has violated their constitutional and statutory rights. A black complainant may be able to prove that a developer has denied him a particular home in order that some white person may acquire it. Undoubtedly, that racial differentiation has immediately injured a member of a disadvantaged minority group. Yet, a likely effect of any other course would be the creation or extension of the isolated minority ghetto to the detriment of those who live there and, in the long run, to the detriment of the entire community.

This situation presents sharply and clearly the question whether injurious discriminatory treatment of an individual because of his race necessarily offends the constitutional concept of equal protection of the laws. If our Constitution and laws mean that disadvantage imposed through racially based disparity of treatment is always illegal, that is the end of the matter. We have, however, seen that courts have permitted legislatures and school boards to act voluntarily to achieve districtwide racial balance in public school enrollment.[41] Similarly, in the employment cases, courts of appeals have sanctioned racial hiring quotas adopted to remedy racial exclusion from employment.[42] For present

---

40. Navasky, *The Benevolent Housing Quota,* 6 How. L.J. 30, 34-35 (1960); Weaver, *Integration in Public Housing,* in 256 ANNALS 86 (1956).
41. *See* notes 21, 23 *supra.*
42. *See* note 29 *supra.*

purposes these cases seem to say that differences in the treatment of racial groups, like burdensome nonracial discriminatory classifications,[43] are not illegal per se. True, they are suspect, if only because in most circumstances they are oppressive and demeaning, irrelevant to any legitimate public objective, or both.[44] Nonetheless, when they do not disparage or oppress a racial group and indeed serve the purpose of correcting some invidious racial discrimination, the courts have rather consistently sanctioned their remedial use. Because the exclusion of a black under a benign housing quota is neither racially derogatory nor demeaning and the person excluded, though immediately disadvantaged, shares the group interest that the quota serves in aborting a ghetto, his claim that benign housing quotas deny him equal protection of the law seems no stronger, and may be weaker, than the claim of a white job applicant against a preference accorded black job applicants.

At this point it may be helpful to speak briefly about a legal conception that is relevant to the entire subject we are discussing. In common law tradition rights inhere in individuals rather than groups. Moreover, the equal protection clause and typical antidiscrimination statutes in terms forbid certain types of discrimination against the individual. Thus, whenever the operation of any racial quota or racial preference places a racial group at a disadvantage, normally an allegedly injured individual is the person who sues and may be entitled to relief.[45] The underlying concern of the law, however, and indeed the contention that the disadvantaged individual must make and sustain, is that the law should not invidiously or otherwise unfairly single out a class defined by race for burdensome treatment.[46] If this analysis is correct, the validity of the individual's claim depends on the illegality of an underlying scheme that treats racial groups differently. Regarding restricted access to housing, a black claimant can prevail in his challenge to a benign housing quota only if he can invalidate a classification that is intended and well adapted to promote equal treatment for his race.

This brings us to a current and much debated problem of affirma-

---

43. *E.g.*, Williamson v. Lee Optical Co., 348 U.S. 483 (1955).

44. *See* Wright, *The Role of the Supreme Court in a Democratic Society—Judicial Activism or Restraint?* 54 CORNELL L. REV. 1, 18 (1968). Only in the Japanese Exclusion Cases—Korematsu v. United States, 323 U.S. 214 (1944), and Hirabayashi v. United States, 320 U.S. 81 (1943)—has the Court deemed the objective so compelling as to justify oppressive and demeaning racial discrimination.

45. For circumstances in which individual right is decisive against a particular defense, see Missouri *ex rel.* Sipuel v. Board of Regents, 332 U.S. 631, 633 (1948); Gaines v. Canada, 305 U.S. 337, 351 (1938).

46. "Racial discrimination is, by definition, class discrimination . . . [A]lthough the actual effects may . . . vary through the class, the existence of the discriminatory policy threatens the entire class." Hall v. Wertham Bag Co., 251 F. Supp. 184, 186 (M.D. Tenn. 1966). Recognizing this, federal courts permit individual plaintiffs to maintain such suits as class actions. *E.g.*, Evans v. Sheraton Park Hotel, 503 F.2d 177, 188 (D.C. Cir. 1974); Bowe v. Colgate-Palmolive Co., 416 F.2d 711, 719 (7th Cir. 1969); Dickerson v. United States Steel Corp., 64 F.R.D. 351, 357 (E.D. Pa. 1974).

tive action that is typified by the *DeFunis* controversy.[47] A member of the dominant majority complains that a college or university in its process of selecting applicants for admission has accorded a racially discriminatory advantage to a minority group. Of course, it is common knowledge that colleges and universities rarely select entering classes solely on the basis of the relative academic achievements, past or predicted, of the applicants. Veterans, athletes, children of alumni, and other classes are often accorded some degree of special and preferential treatment. Although these preferences have their detractors as well as supporters in academia, the recent emergence of preferential treatment for racial minority applicants seems to cause greatest concern at this time. Now this controversy, like so many of our mundane disputes, is becoming grist for grinding by lawyers and judges.

An unsuccessful white applicant alleges, and for present purposes we assume can prove, that a racial preference accorded minority applicants has resulted in the rejection of his application and the selection of minority applicants whose academic credentials are inferior to his. As commentators have observed,[48] a member of the dominant majority who thus complains of so-called "reverse discrimination" cannot show that the discrimination is racially disparaging, demeaning, or insulting to the majority group, though it is damaging to him. He cannot show that it tends to keep his racial group in or tends to relegate it to a subordinate position in our society.[49] Certainly, this consideration, absent here, has been important in the separate school cases, in the area of residential segregation, and in employment cases in which the courts have viewed discrimination against blacks as a persisting badge of long since outlawed slave status. Moreover, the cases already considered show that a state or a public institution may voluntarily pursue the goal of racial integration and balance farther than the constitutional equal protection concept requires.

That does not, however, relieve the university of the very substantial burden of showing that a racial preference is fair and reasonable and

---

47. DeFunis v. Odegaard, 82 Wash. 2d 11, 507 P.2d 1169 (1973), *vacated as moot*, 416 U.S. 312 (1974). Distinguished professors presented opposing views to the Supreme Court on this controversy as amici curiae. *See* republications of briefs of Archibald Cox, Alexander M. Bickel, & Philip B. Kurland, in *DeFunis is Moot—The Issue Is Not*, LEARNING AND THE LAW, Summer, 1974, at 16. *See also* Flaherty & Sheard, *DeFunis, The Equal Protection Dilemma*, 12 DUQUESNE L. REV. 745 (1974); O'Neil, *Preferential Admission: Equalizing Access of Minority Groups to Higher Education*, 80 YALE L.J. 699 (1971); Redish, *Preferential Law School Admissions and the Equal Protection Clause: An Analysis of Competing Arguments*, 22 U.C.L.A.L. REV. 343 (1974); Note, *Ameliorative Racial Classifications Under the Equal Protection Clause*: DeFunis v. Odegaard, 1973 DUKE L.J. 1126.

48. *E.g.*, Wright, *supra* note 44; *Developments in the Law—Equal Protection*, 82 HARV. L. REV. 1065, 1127 (1969). In a few situations, particularly in the benign housing quota context, the same is true of a minority complainant.

49. In the *DeFunis* case the Supreme Court of Washington stressed this consideration. *See* 82 Wash. 2d 11, 27, 507 P.2d 1169, 1179 (1973).

that it is needed for the accomplishment of some important educational objective.[50] In this connection one must consider both the legitimate goals and purposes of the institution and the details of its selection process. Many colleges and universities that have not discriminated against minority applicants in their past admission policies and practices have, nevertheless, become concerned because they have been admitting very few minority students. This concern has resulted in the adoption of affirmative action programs, ranging from special recruitment programs to modified criteria for admission, all designed to achieve substantial increases in minority enrollment. These types of affirmative action present two questions: whether the objective of increasing minority enrollment is one that state institutions may properly pursue even though some decrease in majority admissions may result, and whether particular schemes for achieving that objective are legitimate.

College and university students are young adults who are approaching and preparing for the time when they will find places and perform roles in an ethnically pluralistic society. Race relations and other problems that grow out of that pluralism are among the most serious and intractable concerns of our contemporary society. Many competent educators and other skilled observers believe that learning with, from, and about each other in and out of the classroom is one of the most valuable features of students' education. In this view association and communication between majority and minority persons within the peer group of students can promote a wholesome outlook and constructive understanding of our society and of the relation between the subject matter of particular academic disciplines and the realities of contemporary life.[51] Thus, for many institutions a substantial increase in minority enrollment is an objective the achievement of which is reasonably calculated to enrich and improve the educational process.[52] The legitimacy of this educational goal seems undeniable.[53] The much harder problem is to distinguish between legally permissible and legally intolerable ways of achieving it.

If there are more qualified applicants than an institution wishes to or can accept, the admissions process must involve two not entirely

---

50. How persuasive this showing must be may depend, formally at least, on the court's choice among several standards of review. See the elaborate discussion in Redish, *supra* note 47, at 350-70.

51. *See* REPORT OF THE PRESIDENT'S COMMISSION ON CAMPUS UNREST 104-16 (1970); CARNEGIE COMMISSION ON HIGHER EDUCATION, A CHANCE TO LEARN: AN ACTION AGENDA FOR EQUAL OPPORTUNITY IN HIGHER EDUCATION 3 (1970). A student body of wide geographic distribution and one that includes foreign students may similarly be deemed educationally valuable.

52. This seems to be the purport of Chief Justice Burger's statement in the Charlotte-Mecklenburg public school case, *supra* note 21. See 402 U.S. at 16.

53. Other goals, such as servicing a community need for more minority persons in particular fields for which higher education is a prerequisite as well as compensating for past minority subordination have been suggested, but they seem less compelling in the present context than the goal of improving education for all.

separable determinations: whether an applicant is eligible or qualified for admission and, if so, whether he should be selected over other qualified applicants.

Beyond satisfying formal prerequisites for admission, admission is likely to depend on the professional judgment of admissions officers, informed by data and comment about the applicant, regarding whether the applicant can cope successfully with the academic requirements of the faculty in the course of study he wishes to pursue. Qualification or eligibility determined in this manner has nothing to do with race. Because race is irrelevant in this context, a lawyer would be hard put to avoid the conclusion that the imposition of higher qualification requirements for members of one race than another is arbitrary and thus, at least in the case of a state university, a denial of equal protection of the laws.

This suggests the desirability and importance of admissions procedures that clearly distinguish the determination of qualification from the complex matter of ultimate selection among the qualified. An institution could demonstrate its observance of this distinction by first establishing a pool of all qualified applicants before deciding to admit any particular applicant. Undoubtedly there are other less formal ways of respecting this distinction. In any event, the first task of the institution whose minority admissions practices are challenged is to show that without regard to race all applicants it accepts are qualified. Thereafter, one can examine the separate and distinct problem of whatever use the institution makes of race in selecting among qualified applicants.

An institution may precipitate a test case by a decision to grant admission free of competition with majority applicants to qualified minority applicants, up to a number not to exceed a predetermined percentage of the entering class that is deemed sufficient to provide a desired substantial racial mix. If then the goal of a substantial racial mix is educationally justifiable, and if the translation of that goal into a particular percentage has not been arbitrary, the one remaining problem seems to be whether demonstrable need for and gain anticipated from acceleration of movement toward the goal makes reasonable, for the time being, the implementing expedient of racial preference in the selection of part of the entering class.

In principle this testing situation is rather similar to the housing and employment racial goal and quota cases. True, the educational objective here, although appropriate, may be less compelling than the objective of promptly eliminating the consequences of invidious past employment discrimination. Nevertheless, even in the area of fair employment practices, the most recent Supreme Court decision on minority preference seems to indicate that the justification need not be the eradication of consequences of the employer's past unfair practices. In

Morton v. Mancari,[54] decided by the Court less than a year ago, white employees of the Bureau of Indian Affairs had complained that the Bureau was granting Indians an ethnic preference in appointments to vacant positions. Moreover, a federal statute[55] and implementing administrative directives required this preference. Yet, a unanimous Court found this requirement fair and reasonable enough to withstand constitutional challenge.[56] If that decision is not a doctrinal abnormality peculiar to the administration of Indian affairs, one is hard pressed to find any principled difference between it and our hypothetical testing case of minority preference in college and university admissions.

To date the large number of denials of certiorari to review minority preference decisions, most notably in fair employment cases,[57] may indicate the willingness of the Supreme Court to abide by the pattern of approval of these preferences that is developing in the lower courts. In addition, the Court's recent approval of the Indian employment preference in *Morton v. Mancari* may provide an even more revealing clue to the future course of authoritative decision. The cases do not suggest that institutions must grant any racial preference, absent persisting consequences of past invidious discrimination, or even that it is always wise. The courts have, however, found preference constitutionally permissible in many situations and even compelled in sufficiently egregious circumstances.[58]

This analysis suggests that there may be merit in the following tentative conclusions about racially preferential admissions of students. First, the use of race as a determinant of the eligibility or qualification of an applicant for college or graduate admission offends the equal protection clause. Second, an institution may legitimately take into account a large number of considerations in addition to academic achievement in the selection of an entering class from a diverse group of eligible and qualified applicants. Third, in this process legitimate educational objectives will often justify the inclusion of membership in a minority group among the considerations taken into account as a significant positive factor. Fourth, beyond the identification of legitimate considerations the detailed administration of the selection process, including the way and extent to which minority goals shall influence choice, requires professional expertise and judgment that is informed by both general and particular experience. Finally, when a result of this process is challenged

---

54. 417 U.S. 535 (1974); *cf*. Porcelli v. Titus, 431 F.2d 1254 (3d Cir. 1970), *cert. denied*, 402 U.S. 944 (1971).

55. Indian Reorganization Act of 1934, § 12, 25 U.S.C. § 472 (1970).

56. Because the allegedly offending employer was the United States rather than a state or local government, the complaint was based on a fifth amendment substantive due process equivalent of fourteenth amendment equal protection. *See* Bolling v. Sharpe, 347 U.S. 497 (1954).

57. Several examples appear in notes 27, 29 *supra*.

58. *See* note 29 *supra*; Castro v. Beecher, 459 F.2d 725 (1st Cir. 1972).

in court, it is doubtful whether a judge should or satisfactorily can do more than determine whether an institution has recognized and weighed legitimate competing considerations, and whether the weight assigned to minority status in a given circumstance is no greater than objective and unbiased professionals in education could reasonably consider essential to the effective pursuit of important educational objectives.

In the meantime legal practitioners, teachers, and students will continue to develop their own perceptions of what the law is, what it is becoming, and what it ought to be in a variety of affirmative action situations. I can only hope that this lecture may stimulate and in some small way aid that process.

The Judicial Quest for Penal Justice: The Warren Court and the Criminal Cases

FRANCIS A. ALLEN

For those who have lived through the era, it is difficult to realize that a generation has grown to maturity since Earl Warren received his commission as Chief Justice of the United States, and that a half-decade and more has elapsed since he relinquished the duties of that office. Following the Chief Justice's retirement, numerous efforts were made to define and to evaluate the "Warren Court." These efforts produced a wide range of conflicting views.[1] The reasons for this divergence are not hard to find. The Court in the years from 1953 to 1969 dealt with issues basic to American society, issues that evoked controversy and passion when raised, and that, in many instances, continue to reverberate in the public forum.

The diversity of views about the Warren Court involves more than disagreements on the values asserted in its decisions or the style that the Court displayed in performing its functions. The very concept of a "Warren Court" is uncertain and elusive. From September, 1953, when Earl Warren first assumed his duties on the Court, until May, 1969, when he resigned, seventeen judges sat on the Court, a group distinctive for its diversity in experience, outlook, and talent.[2] Moreover, the impression one gets from these years is affected by one's interests and by the segments of the Court's work that have attracted his concerns. These impressions vary depending on whether one associates the Warren Court primarily with its contributions to the law of race relations and to more

1. A. BICKEL, THE SUPREME COURT AND THE IDEA OF PROGRESS (1970); A. BICKEL, POLITICS AND THE WARREN COURT (1965); F. GRAHAM, THE SELF-INFLICTED WOUND (1970); P. KURLAND, POLITICS, THE CONSTITUTIONS, AND THE WARREN COURT (1970); Wright, *Professor Bickel, the Scholarly Tradition, and the Supreme Court*, 84 HARV. L. REV. 769 (1971); *Symposium: The Warren Court*, 67 MICH. L. REV. 219 (1968).
2. When Chief Justice Warren was appointed to the Court his colleagues were Justices Black, Reed, Frankfurter, Douglas, Jackson, Burton, Minton, and Clark. Subsequently, he also served with Justices Harlan, Brennan, Whittaker, Stewart, Goldberg, White, Fortas, and Marshall.

generalized problems of equality under the law, or to criminal justice, or to other areas of its docket. During these years there were several "Warren Courts," each with differing life spans. Thus, in the criminal law area it was perhaps not until 1961 and the decision of *Mapp v. Ohio*[3] that a majority of the bench began consistently to reflect those positions that one today considers distinctive of the Warren Court.[4] Although the evidence is less clear, the Warren Court in the criminal cases came to an end a year or two before Chief Justice Warren stepped down. In the area of race relations, on the other hand, the new Chief Justice was confronted by *Brown v. Board of Education*[5] in his first year on the bench; and the movement for racial liberation presented issues that commanded the Court's attention throughout his entire tenure.[6]

The Warren Court, then, is a complex phenomenon, and one that is still capable of engendering controversy and emotion. Underlying the polemics, however, is a common acceptance of the significance of the phenomenon. The history of the Supreme Court during the years in question is widely believed to afford significant evidence about the nature of American society, its political and legal institutions, its values, and its pathologies. This conviction leads one to anticipate that the Warren Court, however defined or appraised, will continue to be an object of inquiry and reflection in the years ahead.

In the sixteen years of Chief Justice Warren's tenure, the Supreme Court decided upwards of 600 criminal cases.[7] Yet the reputation of the Warren Court for judicial activism in the criminal area—as a tribunal dedicated to the enhancement of the rights of defendants and to the expansion of federal judicial authority—rests largely on the results reached and the opinions rendered in hardly more than two dozen

---

3.   367 U.S. 643 (1961).

4.   This view, of course, can be challenged, perhaps most effectively by reference to Griffin v. Illinois, 351 U.S. 12 (1956), dealing with appeal rights of indigent convicted defendants, and the line of cases built upon the *Griffin* precedent, such as Eskridge v. Washington State Board, 357 U.S. 214 (1958). Although *Griffin* foreshadowed some of the characteristic positions of the later Warren Court, it was only some years after its decision that a majority of the Court consistently took positions now regarded as characteristic of the Warren Court. Other important earlier decisions include Silverman v. United States, 365 U.S. 505 (1961); Monroe v. Pape, 365 U.S. 167 (1961); Spano v. New York, 360 U.S. 315 (1959); Sherman v. United States, 356 U.S. 369 (1958); Mallory v. United States, 354 U.S. 449 (1957).

5.   347 U.S. 483 (1954).

6.   See, e.g., Monroe v. Board of Commissioners, 391 U.S. 450 (1968); Loving v. Virginia, 388 U.S. 1 (1967); Rogers v. Paul, 382 U.S. 198 (1965); Goss v. Board of Education, 373 U.S. 683 (1963); Cooper v. Aaron, 358 U.S. 1 (1958).

7.   The statement presupposes a definition of a "criminal case." As used here, a criminal case is one that resulted in a full opinion in the Supreme Court. Per curiam decisions are included if the Court or a member of the Court filed an opinion. If the same majority opinion covered several cases, they are treated as a single case. In addition to cases on direct review, the definition includes habeas corpus and other post-conviction adjudications and those involving criminal contempt judgments that arose out of grand jury or other proceedings closely related to the criminal process. Obviously, a very different total results if different criteria are employed.

cases.[8] In addition to these cases, another group of adjudications, some presenting significant constitutional issues, relate to concerns that only incidentally involve the administration of criminal justice. These cases focus more upon the limitations of the government's substantive powers than procedural safeguards. Included in this category are cases dealing with the definitions of obscenity[9] and the restraints imposed by the first amendment on government efforts to combat political subversion.[10] Cases dealing with the criminal jurisdiction of courts-martial over civilians residing on military installations are also includable in this category.[11] Still another noteworthy group of decisions focused upon procedural issues in noncriminal contexts; they include the important line of decisions dealing with the procedures of Congressional investigations[12] and those decisions concerned with the assertion of rights to conscientious-objector or ministerial status by persons caught up in the military draft.[13] But by far the larger part of the Court's work in the criminal area are the cases in which it was concerned with the routine judicial function of supervising the federal system of criminal justice. Here one finds the Court interpreting federal legislation[14] and the Federal Rules of Criminal Procedure[15] or devising rules of evidence.[16] In addition, the Court was engaged in such tasks as stating the requirement for "net

8. Although some disagreement about the inclusion or exclusion of certain cases would result from compilation of any such list, fair unanimity likely exists on the inclusion of the following: Katz v. United States, 389 U.S. 347 (1967); United States v. Wade, 388 U.S. 218 (1967); *In re* Gault, 387 U.S. 1 (1967); Miranda v. Arizona, 384 U.S. 436 (1966); Escobedo v. Illinois, 378 U.S. 478 (1964); Malloy v. Hogan, 378 U.S. 1 (1964); Fay v. Noia, 372 U.S. 391 (1963); Gideon v. Wainwright, 372 U.S. 335 (1963); Mapp v. Ohio, 367 U.S. 643 (1961). A number of other cases would probably also be included, such as: Duncan v. Louisiana, 391 U.S. 145 (1968); Linkletter v. Walker, 381 U.S. 618 (1965); Griffin v. California, 380 U.S. 609 (1965).

9. Jacobellis v. Ohio, 378 U.S. 184 (1964); Bantam Books, Inc. v. Sullivan, 272 U.S. 58 (1963); Smith v. California, 361 U.S. 147 (1959); Roth v. United States, 354 U.S. 476 (1957); Butler v. Michigan, 352 U.S. 380 (1957).

10. United States v. Robel, 389 U.S. 258 (1967); Scales v. United States, 367 U.S. 203 (1961); Yates v. United States, 354 U.S. 298 (1957).

11. Kinsella v. United States *ex rel.* Singleton, 361 U.S. 234 (1960); Reid v. Covert, 354 U.S. 1 (1957); Reid v. Covert, 351 U.S. 487 (1956); Kinsella v. Krueger, 351 U.S. 470 (1956); United States *ex rel.* Toth v. Quarles, 350 U.S. 11 (1955).

12. Yellin v. United States, 374 U.S. 109 (1963); Deutch v. United States, 367 U.S. 456 (1961); Barenblatt v. United States, 360 U.S. 109 (1959); Sacher v. United States, 356 U.S. 576 (1958); Watkins v. United States, 354 U.S. 178 (1957); Emspack v. United States, 349 U.S. 190 (1955); Quinn v. United States, 349 U.S. 155 (1955).

13. Gonzales v. United States, 364 U.S. 59 (1960); Witmer v. United States, 348 U.S. 375 (1955); Dickinson v. United States, 346 U.S. 389 (1953).

14. Wyatt v. United States, 362 U.S. 525 (1960); Hawkins v. United States, 358 U.S. 74 (1958); Jencks v. United States, 353 U.S. 657 (1957).

15. United States v. Fabrizio, 385 U.S. 263 (1966); Gilbert v. United States, 370 U.S. 650 (1962); United States v. Turley, 352 U.S. 407 (1957); United States v. Howard, 352 U.S. 212 (1957); United States v. Bramblett, 348 U.S. 503 (1955); United States v. Five Gambling Devices, 346 U.S. 441 (1953).

16. Harris v. United States, 382 U.S. 162 (1965); United States v. Behrens, 375 U.S. 162 (1963); Schaffer v. United States, 362 U.S. 511 (1960); Heflin v. United States, 358 U.S. 415 (1959); Lemke v. United States, 346 U.S. 325 (1953).

worth" tax prosecutions,[17] dealing with the problem of the proper "unit of prosecution" when several criminal provisions are violated by the same course of conduct,[18] and laying down the requisites of in forma pauperis appeals in the federal system.[19] In estimating the importance of various aspects of the Court's work, a purely quantitative measure is, of course, inappropriate. Yet it is well to remember as one considers the Court's performance in the highly publicized and controversial cases, that while these cases were under consideration, the Court was week by week disposing of less dramatic issues involving the decency and efficiency of the criminal process. The cumulative importance of this latter activity is very great, and its actual impact may well rival that of the more celebrated adjudications.

There was a time when college students received instruction on the principle of continuity in history. History, it was said, is a continuous stream of events with no abrupt turns or sudden changes. The implication of this proposition for the matters under consideration is that the performance of the Warren Court in the criminal cases has both prologue and epilogue. Contemporary commentary suggests that some persons are unaware that the Supreme Court had concerned itself with establishing constitutional minima for state systems of criminal justice long before the Warren Court came into existence. In fact, this effort had constituted a major concern of the Court for 30 years before Earl Warren took the oath as Chief Justice.[20] Although the origins of a complex body of constitutional doctrine can rarely be fully identified, for practical purposes the modern law of constitutional criminal procedure begins, not in 1953 when the Warren judicial tenure commenced or even when the Warren Court began to speak in its own distinctive tones, but rather in 1932 with the decision in the great case of *Powell v. Alabama.*[21] In *Powell* the Court for the first time interpreted the due process clause of the fourteenth amendment to include rights of counsel in state criminal proceedings.

17. United States v. Massei, 355 U.S. 595 (1958); Friedburg v. United States, 348 U.S. 142 (1954); Holland v. United States, 348 U.S. 121 (1954).
18. Harris v. United States, 359 U.S. 19 (1959); Lader v. United States, 358 U.S. 169 (1958); Gore v. United States, 357 U.S. 386 (1958); Prince v. United States, 352 U.S. 322 (1957); Bell v. United States, 349 U.S. 81 (1955).
19. Coppedge v. United States, 269 U.S. 438 (1962).
20. A considerable literature appeared concerning this earlier period. *See, e.g.,* Allen, *The Wolf Case: Search and Seizure, Federalism, and the Civil Liberties,* 45 ILL. L. REV. 1 (1950); Boskey & Pickering, *Federal Restrictions on State Criminal Procedure,* 13 U. CHI. L. REV. 266 (1946); Hall, *Police and Law in a Democratic Society,* 28 IND. L.J. 133 (1953); Inbau, *The Confession Dilemma in the United States Supreme Court,* 43 ILL. L. REV. 442 (1948); McCormick, *Some Problems and Developments in the Admissibility of Confessions,* 24 TEX. L. REV. 239 (1946); Paulsen, *The Fourteenth Amendment and the Third Degree,* 6 STAN. L. REV. 411 (1954); Scott, *Federal Restrictions on Evidence in State Criminal Cases,* 34 MINN. L. REV. 489 (1950).
21. 287 U.S. 45 (1932). Evidence of the Court's new concern for the problems of state criminal procedure is apparent as early as Moore v. Dempsey, 261 U.S. 86 (1923).

One of the intriguing questions of our constitutional history is why the Court in the 1930's, under the aegis of the due process clause, first undertook to impose limitations on state power in the administration of criminal justice. The *Powell* case, after all, was decided more than 60 years after the fourteenth amendment became part of the Constitution. In those earlier years the Court was not wholly silent on the relations of the fourteenth amendment to state criminal justice. What is significant about these adjudications, however, is that in each case the claim of individual right against state authority was rejected by the Court, and state volition in the administration of criminal justice was left virtually untouched.[22]

The reasons for the Court's new conception of the uses of the due process clause as it emerged in *Powell* and in scores of cases that followed have invited speculation.[23] If the question is put more broadly, however, the modern concern with problems of criminal justice appears natural and even inevitable. A crisis in freedom has afflicted western societies since the First World War, and anxiety about the proper containment of the public force exerted through systems of criminal justice has been widely felt. The *Powell* case was decided in a period when totalitarian regimes were forming in western Europe. It is an interesting coincidence that *Powell v. Alabama* was decided within a few months of Hitler's rise to power in Germany. The European dictatorships, once installed, taught graphic lessons in the uses of the institutions of criminal justice as instrumentalities for the systematic destruction of political values upon which free societies rest.[24] The impact of these events was felt in the United States. One can safely assume that some public officials, including judges, were led to view the regulation of criminal justice functions not as a matter of local concern, but rather as part of the essential strategy of freedom.

Since the Second World War the involvement of criminal justice in the central concerns of American life has increased rather than abated. To a remarkable degree the issues that have divided and agitated us in the past two decades have assumed their most concrete forms and have appeared in sharpest focus within the context of the criminal law and its applications. Fundamental questions about the nature of political obligation, fidelity to law, and the emancipation of conscience from legal restraints reappeared in the 1960's. These questions were made inescapable by criminal prosecutions of those who set themselves against the Viet Nam War or involved themselves in racial militancy. Closely related

---

22. Twining v. New Jersey, 211 U.S. 78 (1908); Maxwell v. Dow, 176 U.S. 581 (1900); Hurtado v. California, 110 U.S. 516 (1884).

23. A more detailed discussion of this question is contained in Allen, *The Supreme Court and State Criminal Justice*, 4 Wayne L. Rev. 191 (1958). *See also* W. Beany, The Right to Counsel in American Courts 156-67 (1955).

24. *See* F. Allen, The Crimes of Politics 4 (1974).

to these issues are the allegations of inequalities and inequities in American society. These charges have not been confined to the criminal law, but, on the contrary, have encompassed nearly every aspect of our social arrangements. But charges of inequality possess an even sharper bite when they are hurled at a system that employs as its sanctions the deprivation of property, of liberty, and, on occasion, of life itself.

Finally, the administration of criminal justice has held a place of central concern in the modern world because of the insecurity and apprehensions produced by the widespread conviction that serious crime is increasing in this country. We have again seen that fears of crime and of the collapse of public order are a powerful political dynamic in American society, a perception that appears to have sometimes eluded practitioners of liberal politics.[25]

An argument can thus be stated for the importance of the criminal justice process in the 20th century world. Less clear, however, is the reason why problems of regulating the uses of governmental power in the criminal process have become so predominantly a matter of judicial concern in the United States. In no other western society has the regulation of police and prosecutorial officials, as well as the functioning of the courts, been understood in comparable degree to be a function of judges. In no other nation has so large and intricate a corpus of constitutional doctrine emerged relating to the functioning of criminal justice as that created or influenced by the Supreme Court of the United States.[26] The reasons surely do not reside in any peculiar qualifications of American judges or any unusual adaptability of American courts for the task, especially that part of the task that relates to the oversight of nonjudicial officers performing official functions outside of Court. On the contrary, the courts operate under severe and inherent limitations of means and resources for the task. One devising institutions for Utopia would not likely delegate so large a responsibility for maintaining the integrity of the criminal justice process to the courts. Ascertaining the reasons for this allocation of responsibilities, as well as the resultant consequences, is important to an understanding and evaluation of the Warren Court's posture in the criminal cases. The questions are perplexing and perhaps defy completely satisfactory answers. One is tempted to say that the Court has taken the initiative in regulating the exercise of government power in systems of criminal justice because of an American propensity to delegate to courts the resolution of great public issues that are agitating society at any particular moment. Given the breadth and adaptability of the great moral imperatives of our Constitution such as due process of law and the equal protection of the laws, few significant public issues cannot be restated in a form apparently consistent

25. *Id.* at 13-14.
26. A sense of these differences is conveyed by POLICE POWER AND INDIVIDUAL FREEDOM (C. Sowle ed. 1962).

with constitutional adjudication. This phenomenon was noted by de Tocqueville almost a century and one half ago and was once again demonstrated in the Watergate crisis.[27]

Part of the reason for the high degree of judicial involvement in the regulation of the criminal process, however, may stem from certain aspects of the criminal justice system in the United States. One of the outstanding characteristics of American criminal justice is the remarkable fragmentation of the system. In a large metropolitan area as many as 100 separate police systems operate, each largely independent of the other.[28] Although the powers of regulation over local prosecution possessed by the state attorney general vary from jurisdiction to jurisdiction, the local prosecutor is typically a publicly elected official with an independent power base who is consequently able to resist efforts at meaningful scrutiny and direction from above. In these circumstances no state prosecutory policy exists, except as may accidentally arise out of the like-mindedness of the officials involved.[29] In addition, some jurisdictions have failed to establish centralized supervision of local jails and lockups even though the interests of public health and safety require it.[30] Admittedly, local police forces are expected to be accountable to the agencies of local government that create and maintain them. In reality, however, one of the striking characteristics of American police agencies, both at the state and federal level, is the degree to which they have succeeded at eluding genuine accountability to civil authority. Indeed, the upper levels of the police hierarchy itself are often unable to maintain effective supervision over the lower levels.[31]

All of this is in sharp contrast to the situation existing in some countries. The ministry of justice, with its broad powers of supervision and coordination, is familiar to continental nations, but is unknown in

27. De Tocqueville observed in 1835: "Scarcely any political question arises in the United States that is not resolved, sooner or later, into a judicial question." 1 DEMOCRACY IN AMERICA 280 (P. Bradley ed. 1948). *See also* United States v. Nixon, 418 U.S. 683 (1974).

28. Some 10 years ago nearly 40,000 separate and independent police units existed in the United States. In a 50-mile radius of Chicago there were approximately 350 municipal, county, and state police forces. R. CALDWELL, CRIMINOLOGY 309 (2d ed. 1965). *See* Note, *Disorganization of Metropolitan Law Enforcement and Some Proposed Solutions*, 43 J. CRIM. L.C. & P.S. 63 (1952).

29. The situation described evoked the following recommendations from the President's Commission on Law Enforcement and Administration of Justice: "States should strengthen the coordination of local prosecution by enhancing the authority of the State attorney general or some other appropriate statewide officer and by establishing a State council on prosecutors comprising all local prosecutors under the leadership of the attorney general." THE PRESIDENT'S COMMISSION ON LAW ENFORCEMENT AND ADMINISTRATION OF JUSTICE, THE CHALLENGE OF CRIME IN A FREE SOCIETY 149 (1967).

30. "Each level of government typically acts independently of the others. . . . Responsibility for the administration of corrections is divided not only among levels of government but also within single jurisdictions." *Id.* at 160.

31. F. ALLEN, *supra* note 24, at 21-22.

the United States.[32] Nothing comparable to the Home Secretary in Great Britain exists here.[33] These institutions may, of course, be wholly inappropriate to American conditions. Some persons have assumed that the fragmentation of American law enforcement avoids the threat to political liberty implicit in a centralized system of internal police. Whether we are in fact free of these dangers is less clear in the light of post-Watergate inquiries into the operations of national police and intelligence agencies. Apart from that controversy, the salient fact remains that in the United States no persons or agencies possess political or administrative responsibility for the decency and efficiency of criminal justice as a whole. We have not been ingenious in devising institutions that subject criminal justice functions to scrutiny and test. This failure to devise alternative institutions charged with such responsibilities explains in part the willingness of American courts to enter these areas. The same fact helps explain the particular forms that judicial intervention has taken.

Commentators have analyzed the Warren Court by identifying its basic ideology—its egalitarian impulse, its involvement with problems of race and poverty, and its libertarian bias.[34] Viewing the Court from other perspectives, however, is also worthwhile. The history of the Warren Court may be taken as a case study of a court that for a season determined to employ its judicial resources in an effort to alter significantly the nature of American criminal justice in the interest of a larger realization of the constitutional ideal of liberty under the law. So viewed, this is surely a history worthy of attention.

Looking back at the Court's treatment of state criminal cases between the decision of *Powell v. Alabama* and the appointment of Earl Warren to the Court, one can easily underestimate the importance of the Court's achievement. In these pre-Warren years the foundations of fourteenth amendment law were laid.[35] The Court's scrutiny of state criminal procedures often resulted in improvements in local criminal processes. Practices relating to the provision of counsel for indigent defendants were liberalized in some states, and the Court's supervision led to a modernization of state post-conviction remedies in several

---

32. *See, e.g.,* THE ROYAL NORWEGIAN MINISTRY OF JUSTICE, ADMINISTRATION OF JUSTICE IN NORWAY (1957). Proposals to create a Ministry of Justice in England are discussed in R. JACKSON, THE MACHINERY OF JUSTICE IN ENGLAND 415-19 (4th ed. 1964).

33. Great Britain's Home Secretary is a cabinet officer with broad responsibilities over law enforcement functions. The Secretary's role nevertheless allows for considerable local autonomy and initiative. *See* R. JACKSON, THE MACHINERY OF JUSTICE IN ENGLAND *passim* (4th ed. 1964). *See also* J. CONLIN, LOCAL AND CENTRAL GOVERNMENT—POLICE ADMINISTRATION 70-73 (1967); R. JACKSON, ENFORCING THE LAW *passim* (1967).

34. *See* P. KURLAND, *supra* note 1, at 98-169.

35. Allen, *The Supreme Court, Federalism, and State Systems of Criminal Justice,* 8 DE PAUL L. REV. 213 (1959); Schaefer, *Federalism and State Criminal Procedure,* 70 HARV. L. REV. 1 (1956). *See also* note 10 *supra.*

jurisdictions.[36] Other constructive reactions followed. Most of these, however, related to the improvement of in-court procedures. The Court's impact on state police practices was far less easy to discern.[37] To those, both on and off the Court, who were eager for a more profound judicial influence on the quality of American criminal justice, a significant change in the assumptions and tactics of the Supreme Court seemed clearly required.

The heart of the problem for judicial activism in the criminal area is not simply that of effecting an expansion of doctrine relating to the rights and immunities of persons against whom the state proceeds. The problem also encompasses the question of how, given the limitations of judicial remedies and devices, judicial power may be effectively exerted to achieve the desired objectives. Stated more graphically: how can a court, however exalted its authority, that stands at the apex of a complex judicial structure exercise its powers so as to achieve a genuine impact on the day-by-day behavior of police, prosecutory, judicial, and correctional officials throughout a nation of two hundred million inhabitants? Anyone who studies carefully the judicial expressions of the Warren Court in the criminal cases comes to the realization that this concern with implementation is never far below the surface. One is unlikely to understand the phenomenon of the Warren Court until he perceives that the persistent motive of the Court is not only to declare the rights of persons confronting state power in the criminal arena, but also to enlarge the exercise of its judicial authority in such fashion as most likely to render those declarations effective. This is surely not to say that concern with remedies and implementation is peculiar to fourteenth amendment law relating to criminal justice or even to constitutional adjudication generally. Such concerns impinge upon and condition judicial lawmaking whenever it occurs. Such problems assumed particularly large proportions for the Court, however, as it considered its role in the criminal cases during the early years of the 1960's and before.

One of the most important obstacles to direct applications of federal power is, of course, the federal system itself. The federal system is one of divided authority that imposes a variety of inhibitions and restraints on the exercise of federal judicial power in areas affecting state institutions and traditions of self-determination. The Court's notions of the obligations of federalism were a strongly limiting influence on its role in the criminal cases during the years before the Warren tenure. A reexamination of important decisions such as *Betts v. Brady*[38] and *Wolf*

---

36. *See, e.g.,* ILL. SUP. CT. R. 26(2); Law of Aug. 4, 1949, ch. 38, § 826-32, [1949] Ill. Laws 722.

37. Allen, *supra* note 23, at 201-04.

38. 316 U.S. 455 (1942). "The practice of the courts of Maryland gives point to the principle that the states should not be straight-jacketed in this respect, by a construction of the Fourteenth Amendment." *Id.* at 472.

v. Colorado[39] demonstrates how important these conceptions were. One would expect that the new activism in the criminal cases would result in redefinitions of the obligations of federalism more favorable to the applications of federal power upon state criminal justice systems; and this, in fact, occurred. A great many facets of the Court's work were affected by this redefinition, but nowhere more importantly than in the new constitutional law "incorporating" provisions of the federal Bill of Rights into the due process clause of the fourteenth amendment. This is a familiar story and need not be detailed here. Suffice it to say that the substance, if not the form, of Justice Black's position in *Adamson v. California*[40] prevailed, and the states, as well as the national government, were made subject to the express provisions of the Bill of Rights and to the accretions of judicial law made by the Court over the years when interpreting those provisions.[41] As often stated by proponents of the prevailing view, citizens confronting state authority are now entitled to something more than "watered-down versions" of the Bill of Rights.[42]

In addition, one might expect the Court to be sensitive to limitations on individuals' access to the courts. The impact of judicial power, after all, depends on the access of persons to the source of that power. Long before the Warren era, the Court struck down state prison rules that prohibited inmates from filing petitions in court as violative of the equal protection clause.[43] One of the most important criminal cases

---

39. 338 U.S. 25 (1949).

40. 332 U.S. 46, 68 (1947).

41. In resolving conflicting claims concerning the meaning of this spacious language, the Court has looked increasingly to the Bill of Rights for guidance; many of the rights guaranteed by the first eight Amendments to the Constitution have been held to be protected against state action by the Due Process Clause of the Fourteenth Amendment.
Duncan v. Louisiana, 391 U.S. 145, 147-48 (1968). *See also* Benton v. Maryland, 395 U.S. 784 (1969); Malloy v. Hogan, 378 U.S. 1 (1964). In his Carpentier Lectures, Justice Black observed:

> Through the processes of selective incorporation the Supreme Court has held that the Fourteenth Amendment guarantees against infringement by the states the liberties of the First Amendment, the Fourth Amendment, the Fifth Amendment's privilege against self-incrimination, the Sixth Amendment's rights to notice, confrontation of witnesses, compulsory process for witnesses, and the assistance of counsel, and the Eighth Amendment's prohibition of cruel and unusual punishments. The Fifth Amendment's provision for just compensation had been applied to the states before the *Palko* decision by an essentially similar process. . . . Obviously, I am not completely happy with the selective incorporation theory since it still leaves to the determination of judges the decision as to which Bill of Rights' provisions are "fundamental" and thus applicable to the states. . . . But the selective incorporation process, as it is now being used, does limit the Supreme Court in the Fourteenth Amendment field to specific Bill of Rights' protections and keeps judges from roaming at will in their own notions of what policies outside the Bill of Rights are desirable and what are not. And it has the virtue of having worked to make most of the Bill of Rights' protections applicable to the states.

A CONSTITUTIONAL FAITH 38-40 (1969). Justice Black made a similar statement in his concurring opinion in Duncan v. Louisiana, 391 U.S. 145, 171 (1968).

42. *See, e.g.*, Malloy v. Hogan, 378 U.S. 1, 10-11 (1964); Ohio *ex rel.* Eaton v. Price, 364 U.S. 263, 275 (1960) (Brennan, J., dissenting).

43. Dowd v. Cook, 340 U.S. 206 (1951); Cochran v. Kansas, 316 U.S. 255 (1942).

decided in the early years of the Warren tenure was *Griffin v. Illinois*.[44] In *Griffin* the Court invalidated a system of criminal appeals in state courts that effectively barred indigent persons from appellate review because of their financial inability to purchase transcripts of the trial courts' proceedings. In announcing the judgment of the Court, Justice Black uttered a proposition that was to be heard again in the later years of the Warren Court: "There can be no equal justice where the kind of trial a man gets depends on the amount of money he has."[45] Decisions in cases like these clearly involve far more than concerns about the implementation of judicial authority. They also reflect the basic egalitarian impulse of the Warren years. Yet one should not overlook that cases expanding rights of counsel and rights of access to the judicial process do more than enlarge the protections of those accused or convicted of crime against unfairness at the hands of the government. These cases also increase the number and range of issues exposed to judicial scrutiny and thus enlarge the occasions for judicial supervision of the criminal process.[46] They may also increase burdens on the judicial machinery to such extent as to threaten the quality of the judicial function; but that is another story.

The purposes served by decisions in cases involving rights of counsel and access to the courts are clear enough. They are even clearer in those cases in which the Court sought to recast and refurbish the federal habeas corpus remedy into a more effective instrument for the direct application of federal judicial power in behalf of persons claiming that state incarceration violated their constitutional immunities. Thus, on a memorable decision day[47] the Court handed down its judgment in *Fay v. Noia*.[48] The decision is a genuine tour de force. The Court, having wearied in its efforts to penetrate the thicket of state procedural law, brushed aside those concepts that had traditionally inhibited the administration of the federal habeas corpus remedy—"adequate state ground," "waiver," "failure to exhaust state remedies"—and held the writ available to any state prisoner who had not "deliberately bypassed" the assertion of his federal rights.[49] In other cases the Court expanded

---

44. 351 U.S. 12 (1956).

45. *Id.* at 19. In *Griffin*, Justice Black did not speak for the Court. The quoted statement was, however, included in the Court's opinion in Douglas v. California, 372 U.S. 353, 355 (1963).

46. Analogously, the body of search and seizure law is overwhelmingly the product of enforcement of the exclusionary rule. *Cf.* Barrett, *Exclusion of Evidence Obtained by Illegal Searches—A Comment on* People v. Cahan, 43 CALIF. L. REV. 565 (1955).

47. In addition to *Fay*, the Court issued its opinions in Douglas v. California, 372 U.S. 353 (1963); Gideon v. Wainwright, 372 U.S. 335 (1963); and Townsend v. Sain, 372 U.S. 293 (1963).

48. 372 U.S. 391 (1963).

49. *Id.* at 439. *See* Bator, *Finality in Criminal Law and Federal Habeas Corpus for State Prisoners*, 76 HARV. L. REV. 441 (1963); Shapiro, *Federal Habeas Corpus: A Study in Massachusetts*, 87 HARV. L. REV. 321 (1973); Note, *Developments in the Law—Federal Habeas Corpus*, 83 HARV. L. REV. 1038 (1970).

application of the writ by liberalizing the use of successive applications and redefining the statutory phrase "in custody."[50]

The Court's sense of the nature and limitations of judicial power, however, and the manner in which those realities affected the form and substance of the Court's work are apparent not only in cases dealing directly with the problem of judicial remedies, but throughout the range of its involvements with criminal justice. The confinement of certain of its new constitutional directives to prospective operation provides an interesting illustration.[51] Traditionally, of course, one of the distinctions between court adjudication and legislative lawmaking is based on the fiction that judges "find" and do not "make" law, and that, consequently, the judicial rule so discovered was in existence before its announcement by a court. In other words, adjudication is retrospective in its effects. As a result, a prisoner is entitled to rely on a new constitutional rule as a ground for his release even though the rule was announced long after his conviction. Legislative lawmaking, on the other hand, ordinarily speaks to the future. Indeed, retrospectivity in legislation is suspect and is even constitutionally forbidden if it falls within the strictures of the ex post facto clause.

The notion of prospectivity of judicial decisions creates unease. This is surely not because of an atavistic affection for a view that denies the reality of judicial lawmaking. One's concerns with prospectivity need not be founded on the assumption that all legal rules pre-exist in some platonic corpus juris, accessible only to priests in judicial robes. The unease is based, in the first instance, on the inequity of persons languishing in prison who have suffered precisely the same deprivations at the hands of government that now invalidate the convictions of those fortunate enough to have run afoul of the law after, not before, the new constitutional rule was made effective. The sense of inequity is heightened by the ineptness and even the necromancy that the Court has displayed in determining which constitutional holdings are subject to the rule of prospectivity[52] and in designating the dates from which the new

---

50. Smith v. Yeager, 393 U.S. 122 (1968); Carafas v. LaVallee, 391 U.S. 234 (1968); Peyton v. Rowe, 391 U.S. 54 (1968); Jones v. Cunningham, 371 U.S. 236 (1963); Sanders v. United States, 373 U.S. 1 (1963).

51. The "prospectivity" controversy has produced an interesting literature. *See, e.g.,* Mishkin, *The High Court, the Great Writ, and the Due Process of Time and Law,* 79 HARV. L. REV. 56 (1965); Schwartz, *Retroactivity, Reliability and Due Process: A Reply to Professor Mishkin,* 33 U. CHI. L. REV. 719 (1966).

52. The Court's increasingly indiscriminate use of the rule of prospectivity has heightened the problems. In Linkletter v. Walker, 381 U.S. 618 (1965), the Court confined the application of the exclusionary rule in search and seizure cases to prospective operation. Whatever the merits of that decision, one must recognize that the Court in Mapp v. Ohio, 367 U.S. 643 (1961), had overturned an important and often fiercely defended policy, a policy that the Court had explicitly validated only a dozen years earlier in Wolf v. Colorado, 338 U.S. 25 (1949). Subsequently, however, the Court applied the prospectivity rule to decisions representing an almost routine incremental growth of constitutional doctrine. *See, e.g.,* Adams v. Illinois, 405 U.S. 278 (1972);

rules are effective.[53] At first glance the prospectivity rule appears to be an act of judicial self-abnegation, for it limits the impact of the new rule to the future. In reality, however, it is a device that encourages the making of new law by reducing some of the social costs. One reason, for example, that a majority of the Court clung so long to *Betts v. Brady*[54] precedent and avoided a rule that would entitle indigent defendants as of right to the appointment of counsel in serious criminal prosecutions, was its anticipated impact on the convictions of thousands of persons already in prison. This is not a matter of speculation. In a 1947 case Justice Frankfurter candidly noted that "such an abrupt innovation as recognition of the constitutional claim here made implies, would furnish opportunities hitherto uncontemplated for opening wide the prison doors of the land."[55] By avoiding the problem of the jail delivery, an activist court is freed in a variety of situations to make new law.[56] Thus, in the prospectivity cases the Court confronted one of the traditional inhibitions associated with the exercise of judicial power and simply eliminated or modified it.

The Court's reactions to the nature and limitations of judicial power were also revealed as it dealt with some of its most "substantive" concerns. Surely one of the most distinctive tendencies of the Warren Court was its allegiance to the adversary theory of criminal justice.[57] Thus, a large part of the Court's work in the criminal area consisted of its efforts to revitalize the adversary process in those parts of the system in which it was always supposed to flourish. Notable illustrations of

---

Williams v. United States, 401 U.S. 646 (1971); Desist v. United States, 394 U.S. 244 (1969). Among the losses incurred is the discouragement of local judicial reform in anticipation of new Supreme Court rules of constitutional law of the sort that occurred in anticipation of the decision of Gideon v. Wainwright, 372 U.S. 335 (1963). Justice Fortas made the point explicitly in his dissent in *Desist*:

> [These decisions] add this Court's approval to those who honor the Constitution's mandate only where acceptable to them or compelled by the precise and inescapable specifics of a decision of this Court. And they award dunce caps to those law enforcement officers, courts, and public officials who do not merely stand by until an inevitable decree issues from this Court, specifically articulating that which is clearly imminent in the fulfillment of the Constitution, but who generously apply the mandates of the Constitution as the developing case law elucidates them.

394 U.S. 244, 277 (1969). *Cf.* People v. Dorado, 62 Cal. 2d 338, 398 P.2d 361, 42 Cal. Rptr. 169 (1965).

53. The extraordinary diversity of rules for locating the start of the period of prospective operation is illustrated by Desist v. United States, 394 U.S. 244 (1969); Johnson v. New Jersey, 384 U.S. 719 (1966); Tehan v. United States ex rel. Shott, 382 U.S. 406 (1966); Linkletter v. Walker, 381 U.S. 618 (1965). For Justice Douglas' comments on the impact of the prospectivity holding applicable to the *Miranda* decision, see his dissenting opinion in *Desist*, 394 U.S. at 255.

54. 316 U.S. 455 (1942).

55. Foster v. Illinois, 332 U.S. 134, 139 (1947).

56. The problem, of course, was not avoided in the counsel cases, for when the *Gideon* decision was reached, it was given retrospective operation. *See* Linkletter v. Walker, 381 U.S. 618, 639 (1965).

57. See the concurring opinion of Justice Goldberg in Hardy v. United States, 375 U.S. 277, 282 (1964).

these efforts include the decisions enlarging the rights to counsel in the criminal trial and the criminal appeal. Even more striking, however, are the cases in which the Court extended the adversary process into areas of the system in which, theretofore, adversary proceedings were unknown or rarely employed. Illustrations encompass recognition of rights to counsel in probation revocation proceedings,[58] in post-conviction procedures,[59] in the juvenile court,[60] and the application of the privilege against self-incrimination, and expansion of rights to counsel in the pretrial stages of criminal proceedings.[61]

Clearly, the Court's attitudes toward the adversary system reflect some of its deepest convictions about the requisites for the realization of constitutional liberty and the proper containment of the coercive powers of government. Even here, however, the Court's enthusiasm for adversary proceedings is based in part on the belief that their wider application will significantly reduce the problems of judicial scrutiny and regulation of the system of criminal justice. Thus, one of the continuing complaints about secret police interrogation of suspects goes beyond the fear that incommunicado questioning gives rise to opportunities and temptations for police abuse. Again and again members of the Court complained that its powers of judicial scrutiny in confession cases are seriously compromised by its inability to know what, in fact, occurred behind closed doors. The observation of Chief Justice Warren in *Miranda v. Arizona* is typical of those in many earlier cases: "Interrogation still takes place in privacy. Privacy results in secrecy and this in turn results in a gap in our knowledge as to what goes on in the interrogation room."[62] There also emerges in the Court's thought the notion of the lawyer, not only as advocate and counsellor, but as a witness of what occurs in proceedings theretofore secret. The Court came to view the attorney's presence as a deterrent to police wrongdoing. Again, these points were made explicitly. Justice Black wrote, for example, in his dissenting opinion in *In re Groban*: "Nothing would be better calculated to prevent misuse of official power in dealing with a witness or suspect than the scrutiny of his lawyer or friends or even of disinterested bystanders."[63] Chief Justice Warren added in *Miranda*: "The presence of a lawyer can also help to guarantee that the accused gives a fully accurate statement to the police and that statement is rightly reported by

58. Mempa v. Rhay, 389 U.S. 128 (1967).
59. Johnson v. Avery, 393 U.S. 483 (1969).
60. *In re* Gault, 387 U.S. 1 (1967).
61. Miranda v. Arizona, 384 U.S. 436 (1966); Escobedo v. Illinois, 378 U.S. 478 (1964).
62. 384 U.S. 436, 448 (1966). *See also* Davis v. North Carolina, 384 U.S. 737, 741 (1966); Gallegos v. Colorado, 370 U.S. 49, 50-1 (1962); Crooker v. California, 357 U.S. 433, 443-45 (1958) (dissenting opinion); Ashcraft v. Tennessee, 322 U.S. 143, 152 (1944).
63. 352 U.S. 330, 342-43 (1957).

the prosecution at trial."[64] The concept of lawyer as witness and regulator of police behavior also figures prominently, of course, in the cases dealing with rights to counsel in police "lineup" procedures.[65]

Perhaps the most interesting influence of the exigencies of judicial supervision in criminal cases on the kinds of judicial lawmaking in which the Court engaged is revealed in the tendency of the Court to turn to broad, legislative-like directives, sometimes called "flat" or "per se" rules.[66] Such a rule is one in which a given fact, circumstances, or a limited set of facts is taken as the requisite ground for reversal in a criminal case or the barring of evidence from court. These rules avoid or lessen the occasions that require consideration of the "totality of the circumstances" presented by the record and the concomitant determination whether, on balance, the defendant received a fair trial in the particular case. The principal advantages of per se rules to a Court embracing broad supervision of the criminal justice function were thought to be two. First, such rules give relatively certain guidance to the lower courts, and thus avoid the confusions and uncertainties associated with precedents that weigh a multitude of factors, some of which may be unique to the particular case at hand.[67] Second, such rules are applicable to a great mass of cases at the trial court levels without direct involvement of the Supreme Court, thereby minimizing the consequences of the Court's lack of time and resources to adjudicate more than the smallest fraction of criminal cases presenting constitutional issues. Justice Black was merely articulating long-held concerns when, in the oral argument of the *Miranda* case, he said: "[I]f you are going to determine [the admissibility of the confession] each time on the circumstances . . . [if] the Court will take them one by one . . . it is more than we are capable of doing."[68]

The most successful of the per se rules is undoubtedly the rule of *Gideon v. Wainwright*.[69] *Gideon* requires the reversal of convictions when defendants did not intelligently waive their right to counsel and

64. 384 U.S. 436, 470 (1966).
65. Stovall v. Denno, 388 U.S. 293 (1967); Gilbert v. California, 388 U.S. 263 (1967); United States v. Wade, 388 U.S. 218 (1967).
66. The Court has employed the "per se" nomenclature. *See* United States v. Wade, 388 U.S. 218, 240 (1967); Miranda v. Arizona, 384 U.S. 436, 544 (1966).
67. A revealing debate on the "certainty" issue occurred in a case decided in the first year of the Warren tenure, Irvine v. California, 347 U.S. 128 (1954). In the course of his dissent, Justice Frankfurter quoted from the concurring opinion of Justice Holmes in Le Roy Fibre Co. v. Chicago, M. & St. P. Ry., 232 U.S. 340, 354 (1914):
It is especially true of the concept of due process that between the difference of degree which that inherently undefinable concept entails "and the simple universality of the rules of the Twelve Tables of Leges Barbarorum, there lies the culture of two thousand years."
347 U.S. at 143.
68. *Quoted in* Kamisar, *A Dissent from the Miranda Dissents*, 65 MICH. L. REV. 59, 103 (1966). *See also* Y. KAMISAR, W. LAFAVE, & J. ISRAEL, MODERN CRIMINAL PROCEDURE 513 (4th ed. 1974).
69. 372 U.S. 335 (1963).

were not represented by counsel. The older rule of *Betts v. Brady*[70] required a wide ranging consideration of factors such as the age, experience, intelligence, and mental condition of the defendant in determining whether he had or had not been denied his constitutional right to a fair trial. Long before *Betts* was formally overruled, the Court had deprived it of vitality,[71] and when, in 1963, *Gideon* came before the Court, the states were eager for change. Twenty-two of them filed amicus briefs urging the Court to replace the *Betts* rule with the more intelligible categorical requirement of the appointment of counsel for indigent defendants in serious criminal cases.[72] Despite practical problems of implementation,[73] the Court has not retreated from *Gideon*. Indeed, the Burger Court expanded the appointment requirement to include all misdemeanor cases in which incarceration is an authorized penalty.[74]

The history of per se rules in the search and seizure area is very different. In *Wolf v. Colorado*[75] the Court announced a "flat" rule of a different sort, one that appeared categorically to exempt state courts from constitutional obligation to bar the admission of illegally seized evidence in criminal trials. Despite Justice Frankfurter's advocacy of a "totality of the circumstances" test that would authorize reversals of state convictions in particularly shocking cases, the Court in *Irvine v. California*[76] rejected this alternative and maintained the *Wolf* precedent in full rigor. Consequently, when the Court decided *Mapp v. Ohio*[77] and imposed the exclusionary rule on the states, there had been no experience with a *Betts*-type rule in the search and seizure area. Conceivably, had there been such an interlude, the result in *Mapp* might have been more warmly welcomed when it came. Although Justice Clark in his opinion for the Court in *Mapp* made much of an "inexorable" shift in state law favorable to the exclusionary rule, that rule when announced was not supported by the consensus that greeted *Gideon v. Wainwright*.[78]

In the area of police interrogation the categorical requirement of

---

70.   316 U.S. 455 (1942).

71.   *See* McNeal v. Culver, 365 U.S. 109 (1961); Hudson v. North Carolina, 363 U.S. 697 (1960). "To continue a rule which is honored by this Court only by lip service is not a healthy thing and in the long run will do disservice to the federal system." Harlan, J., concurring in Gideon v. Wainwright, 372 U.S. 335, 351 (1963).

72.   Gideon v. Wainwright, 372 U.S. 335, 345 (1963).

73.   There is a substantial literature on implementation of rights of counsel. Recent items include Boston University Center for Criminal Justice, The Right to Counsel: The Implementation of *Argersinger v. Hamlin* (1974); Wice & Pilgrim, *Meeting the Gideon Mandate: A Survey of Public Defender Programs*, 58 Judicature 400 (1975).

74.   *See* Argersinger v. Hamlin, 407 U.S. 25 (1972).

75.   338 U.S. 25 (1949).

76.   347 U.S. 128 (1954).

77.   367 U.S. 643 (1961).

78.   372 U.S. 335 (1963). Assertion of a "seemingly inexorable" movement toward the exclusionary rule was first made in Elkins v. United States, 364 U.S. 206, 219 (1960).

the *Miranda* warning was clearly the product of frustration and dissatisfactions experienced in the administration of the confession rule. The problems perceived by the Court to be associated with incommunicado questioning of witnesses and suspects have already been sufficiently canvassed. The affirmance of the conviction in *Stein v. New York*[79] illustrates the paradox that many members of Court objected to: the meticulous and conscientious protection of the accused's privilege against self-incrimination in the courtroom and the extended period of secret police questioning that was allowed to occur without warnings or supervision under circumstances that gave rise to sharply disputed questions of fact regarding the use of violence on the defendant. To many, the procedures resembled a scene from the theater of the absurd.[80]

Other problems, however, proceeed from the "involuntary confession" concept itself. By the 1950's an involuntary confession was most often defined as one obtained from a suspect by "overbearing his will." "The limits in any case," the Court wrote, "depend upon a weighing of the circumstances of pressure against the power of resistance of the person confessing."[81] In virtually all cases in which confessions are obtained through in-custody police questioning, however, it appears that the "circumstances of pressure" prevailed over the suspect's powers of resistance. This observation might suggest that all admissions of guilt, except those that are uttered by the accused without official provocation of any kind, are "involuntary." The Court clearly did not intend that result. The difficulty, interestingly enough, was noted by Justice Harlan in his dissent in *Miranda*: "To speak of any confession of crime made after arrest as being 'voluntary' or 'uncoerced' is somewhat inaccurate . . . ."[82] Again, how does a court weigh "the circumstances of pressure" and estimate their impact on the "power of resistance of the person confessing"? Here a court is required to consider a formidable list of factors relating to the ways in which the interrogation was conducted and to the physical and psychological characteristics of the accused.[83] Even if one assumes that the "facts" presented by the record are reliable, he will lack a calculus to determine whether the pressures generated by the police, given the powers of resistance of the accused, have exceeded the constitutional restraints. The problem, of course, is that modern formulations of the confession rule fail to articulate adequately the issue the Court must resolve. This being true, the Court most

79. 346 U.S. 156 (1953).
80. The classic statement of this view is found in Kamisar, *Equal Justice In the Gatehouses and Mansions of American Criminal Procedure*, in Criminal Justice in Our Time (A. Howard ed. 1965).
81. Fikes v. Alabama, 352 U.S. 191, 197 (1957), quoting Stein v. New York 346 U.S. 156, 185 (1952).
82. 384 U.S. 436, 515 (1966). The difficulty was articulated at least as early as Justice Jackson's dissenting opinion in Ashcraft v. Tennessee, 322 U.S. 143, 156 (1944).
83. *See, e.g.,* Culombe v. Connecticut, 367 U.S. 568 (1961); Spano v. New York, 360 U.S. 315 (1959).

often reached its conclusions on the basis of some total impression of the offensiveness of the police behavior in the circumstances of the particular case. This observation was all but acknowledged by Chief Justice Warren when he wrote: "But neither the likelihood that the confession is untrue nor the preservation of the individual's freedom of will is the sole interest at stake."[84] Clearly, precedents based on such a process of adjudication are unlikely to provide adequate guidance to the lower courts, much less to the police. The impulse to construct more categorical guidelines for large-scale application, therefore, appears at least intelligible.

These, then, have been some of the characteristic facets of the Warren Court during its expansionist phase. It has been suggested that the kind of law made by the Court in that period was strongly conditioned by the exigencies of its effort to provide supervision of state and federal systems of criminal justice through the uses of judicial power. Another significant aspect of this history, however, is the evidence of an ebbing of the activist impulse almost at the point at which it reached its highest level—in *Miranda* and *In re Gault*.[85] No attempt will be made here to account fully for this change of mood and behavior, but brief attention will be given to two aspects of the change: the increasing vulnerability of the exclusionary rule in search and seizure cases and the erosion of the per se rules relating to police interrogation.

The changing attitudes of the Court toward the exclusionary rule in the search and seizure cases is best illustrated by three statements in opinions of the Court made at 7-year intervals. In the course of his remarks in *Irvine v. California*,[86] decided in 1954, Justice Jackson presented a case against the rule. "The disciplinary or educational effect of the court's releasing the defendant for police misbehavior," he wrote, "is so indirect as to be no more than a mild deterrent at best."[87] When, 7 years later, the Court imposed the exclusionary rule on the states, Justice Clark exuberantly described the rule, not only as a constitutionally required deterrent safeguard, but also as one that "makes very good sense."[88] Finally, in Chief Justice Warren's 1968 opinion in *Terry v. Ohio*,[89] a much more measured evaluation is made. The exclusionary rule, he says, cannot reach certain kinds of police behavior. Perhaps the implication was that the Court had not always appraised the rule's limitations realistically.

The vulnerability of the exclusionary rule to constitutional reappraisal today is closely related to the Court's characterizations of the

---

84. Blackburn v. Alabama, 361 U.S. 199, 207 (1960).
85. 387 U.S. 1 (1967). In *Gault* the Court imposed some of the basic assumptions of adversarial justice on the procedures of juvenile courts.
86. 347 U.S. 128 (1954).
87. *Id.* at 136-37.
88. Mapp v. Ohio, 367 U.S. 643, 657 (1961).
89. 392 U.S. 1 (1968).

basis and purposes of the rule as developed in the closing years of the Warren tenure. In these cases the Court tended to view the exclusionary rule solely as an instrumentality to deter police misbehavior. This exclusive reliance on the deterrence rationale probably does not accurately characterize the understanding of the Court in the formative phases of the rule's history.[90] More typical are the comments of Justice Brandeis in *Olmstead v. United States*:[91]

> Our government is the potent, omnipresent teacher. . . . To declare that in the administration of the criminal law the end justifies the means—to declare that the Government may commit crimes in order to secure the conviction of a private criminal—could bring terrible retribution.

Nor was the deterrence factor the only or even the chief mainstay of the Court's argument in *Mapp v. Ohio*. Justice Clark placed considerable reliance on the "imperative of judicial integrity"—that courts not participate in illegality by permitting the fruits of unconstitutional searches to provide the basis for convictions in court.[92] Yet when Justice Clark wrote in *Linkletter v. Walker*,[93] he gave these considerations short shrift; *Mapp* was permitted only prospective operation by reason of a view that almost entirely confined the rule to its supposed deterrent justification. Justice Black, dissenting in that case, denied that the supposed deterrent effects were the basis of the *Mapp* rule and added ". . . if that is the sole purpose, reason, object and effect of the rule, the Court's action in adopting it sounds more like law-making than construing the Constitution."[94] Yet in virtually every case in which characterizations of the rule make a difference in the result reached, the deterrence function prevailed as the sole or at least the predominant justification for the rule.[95]

---

90. The opinion in Weeks v. United States, 232 U.S. 383 (1914), in which the federal rule of exclusion was announced, contains no language that expressly justifies the rule by reference to a supposed deterrent effect on police officials. Thus, the Court said:
The tendency of those who execute the criminal laws of the country to obtain convictions by means of unlawful seizures and enforced confessions . . . should find no sanction in the judgments of the courts which are charged at all times with the support of the Constitution and to which people of all conditions have a right to appeal for the maintenance of such fundamental rights.
Id. at 392. And again:
To sanction such proceedings would be to affirm by judicial decision a manifest neglect if not an open defiance of the prohibitions of the Constitution, intended for the protection of the people against such unauthorized action.
Id. at 394.
91. 277 U.S. 438, 485 (1928).
92. 367 U.S. 643, 659 (1961). *See also* Elkins v. United States, 364 U.S. 206, 222 (1960).
93. 381 U.S. 618 (1965).
94. *Id.* at 649. This view, however, did not inhibit Justice Black, when dissenting from the majority's refusal to apply the harmless error rule, from asserting that "[t]he primary reason the 'exclusionary rule' was adopted by this Court was to deter unreasonable searches and seizures. . . ." Bumper v. North Carolina, 391 U.S. 543, 560 (1968).
95. *See, e.g.*, Alderman v. United States, 394 U.S. 165 (1969) (standing); Linkletter v. Walker, 381 U.S. 618 (1965) (prospectivity); *cf.* Chambers v. Maroney, 399 U.S.

The reason why the deterrence rationale renders the exclusionary rule vulnerable is that the case for the rule as an effective deterrent of police misbehavior has proved, at best, to be an uneasy one. The difficulties of that case were delineated in a well-known essay by Professor Dallin Oaks.[96] Admittedly, subsequent studies have asserted that the evidence may be stronger than the agnosticism of Oaks suggests.[97] Nevertheless, until the rule rests on a principled basis rather than an empirical proposition, the *Mapp* precedent, provided the Court does not overrule or substantially modify it, will remain in a state of unstable equilibrium.[98] The Warren Court failed in its closing years to provide a principled underpinning for the rule.

A second illustration of the Court's changing mood is the history of the *Miranda* rules. The Court's great experiment with per se rules in the *Miranda* case produced much less impact on actual law enforcement practices than either the supporters or opponents of the Court's holding anticipated. In part this was caused by the curiously tentative posture of the opinion itself, particularly with reference to waivers of the rights to silence and of the assistance of counsel.[99] The paradox was pinpointed by one of the dissenters, Justice White. "But if," he asked, "the defendant may not answer without a warning a question such as 'Where were you last night?' without having his answer be a compelled one, how can the Court ever accept his negative answer to the question of whether he wants to consult his retained counsel or counsel whom the court will appoint?"[100] Apparently, however, the Court was content to permit the waiver of *Miranda* rights by the suspect in police custody without the advice of counsel, in the absence of judicial supervision, and with no stated obligations on the part of the police to record the waiver transaction for future judicial scrutiny by electronic or other means. Moreover, as Professor Kamisar has recently reminded us, once the *Miranda* rights of silence and of the assistance of counsel are affirmatively waived, the case has little more to offer.[101] Thus, the same problems of incommunicado police interrogation that produced dissatisfaction and unease in the past, and that led ultimately to the *Miranda* decision itself, continue to exist. The Court might have remedied these defects in the *Miranda*

---

42 (1970) (harmless error); Bumper v. North Carolina, 391 U.S. 543 (1968) (harmless error).

96. Oaks, *Studying the Exclusionary Rule in Search and Seizure*, 37 U. CHI. L. REV. 665 (1970).

97. See, e.g., Canon, *Is the Exclusionary Rule in Failing Health? Some New Data and a Plea Against a Precipitous Conclusion*, 62 KY. L.J. 681 (1973-74); Critique, *On the Limitations of Empirical Evaluations of the Exclusionary Rule: A Critique of the Spiotto Research and United States v. Calandra*, 69 NW. U.L. REV. 740 (1974).

98. *Cf.* United States v. Calandra, 414 U.S. 338 (1974).

99. 384 U.S. 436, 475 (1966).

100. *Id.* at 536.

101. *See* Kamisar, *Kauper's "Judicial Examination of the Accused" Forty Years Later—Some Comments on a Remarkable Article*, 73 MICH. L. REV. 15, 28-29 (1974).

opinion in subsequent judicial reconsideration of the *Miranda* precedent. The Court did not revisit these questions, however, and considerable empirical evidence suggests that the *Miranda* warnings, when given, are rarely sufficient to overcome the "atmosphere of coercion" in custodial interrogation, that the warnings are often not fully understood by the arrested parties, and that a large majority of suspected persons waive their rights to counsel and to remain silent.[102]

The reasons for the loss of impetus by the Warren Court in the closing years of the Chief Justice's tenure are worth a moment's speculation.[103] Sooner or later, of course, a decline in the rate of innovation was inevitable. Throughout the Court's expansionist phase substantial opposition existed within the Court to the course of decisions. Some members opposed most of the principal holdings in this era, and few important cases were decided without sharp dissent.[104] *Gideon v. Wainwright*[105] is one conspicuous exception. A determined minority on the Court, even when it does not prevail, may succeed in reducing the momentum of the majority. There is another possibility considerably more conjectural than the first. Perhaps the late history of the Warren Court suggests that something inherent in the judicial process or the traditions of court adjudication renders it difficult for a court to formulate and to adhere to broad categorical rules that demand the judge to ignore apparently substantial social costs in the form of frustrations of law enforcement in the particular cases under scrutiny. Assurances that the categorical rules do by and large constitute a proper restraint on police activity may often appear remote, speculative, and insufficient to justify the losses sustained in the concrete case.

But surely the most fundamental reasons for the Court's loss of impetus lies in the social and political context of the Court in the late

---

102. Jacobs, *Miranda: The Right to Silence*, 11 TRIAL, March/April, 1975, at 69; Medalie, Zeitz, & Alexander, *Custodial Police Interrogation in Our Nation's Capital: The Attempt to Implement Miranda*, 66 MICH. L. REV. 1347 (1968); Seeburger & Wettick, *Miranda in Pittsburgh—A Statistical Study*, 29 U. PITT. L. REV. 1 (1967); Note, *Interrogations in New Haven: The Impact of Miranda*, 76 YALE L.J. 1519 (1967). *See also* other studies cited in Y. KAMISAR, W. LAFAVE, J. ISRAEL, *supra* note 68, at 592-98.

103. Other evidences of the waning of the Warren Court's impetus are ambiguous but may include the Court's articulation of the harmless error rule in Chapman v. California, 386 U.S. 18 (1967). The appearance of retreat is particularly strong when applied to situations like those involving the Miranda rule, a basic purpose of which was to avoid precisely the sort of scrutiny of the entire record of a case that is demanded by the application of "harmless error" doctrine. *Cf.* People v. Doherty, 67 Cal. 2d 9, 429 P.2d 177 (1967). Another evidence is the Court's termination of the long constitutional debate by upholding the validity of "stop and frisk" in designated circumstances. Terry v. Ohio, 392 U.S. 1 (1968). Further evidence is found in the Court's acceptance of a broad version of the informer's privilege in state cases. *See* McCray v. Illinois, 386 U.S. 300 (1967).

104. Thus, taking *Mapp v. Ohio, Fay v. Noia, Malloy v. Hogan, Escobedo v. Illinois,* and *Miranda v. Arizona* as representative, one finds that in none of these cases were there less than three dissenting votes, and in each there was at least one full-scale dissenting opinion.

105. 372 U.S. 335 (1963).

1960's.[106] That period was a time of social upheaval, violence in the ghettos, and disorder on the campuses. Fears of the breakdown of public order were widespread. Inevitably, the issue of law and order were politically exploited. In the presidential campaign of 1968 the bewildering problems of crime in the United States were represented simply as a war between the "peace forces" and the "criminal forces."[107] The decision in *Miranda* evoked a chorus of criticism of the Court, ranging from the excited to the psychotic.[108] Congress responded with the Omnibus Crime Control and Safe Streets Act of 1968,[109] some provisions of which were obviously retaliatory. These events combined to create an atmosphere that, to say the least, was unfavorable to the continued vitality of the Warren Court's mission in criminal cases.

How is the record of the Warren Court in the criminal cases to be appraised? What is its continuing influence likely to be? One cannot give final answers to these questions because the impact of that Court is part of a still evolving history. Undoubtedly it was an important phenomenon. Whatever diversions or retreats from the precedents of the Warren era are achieved by the Burger Court or future Courts, one can be sure that the status quo ante will not be restored. By reason of what the Warren Court said and did, we now perceive as problems what too often were not seen as problems before. This is the dynamic of change, and that fact may well be more significant than many of the solutions proposed by the Warren Court. The critique of American criminal justice implicit in the opinions of the Warren era was essentially ethical. Barring cataclysmic upheavals in American life even more devastating than those we anticipate, one expects this ethical insight to persist and to provide guidance in the years ahead.

It is important, however, not to canonize the Warren Court and not to regard its works as sacrosanct. It was often wrong and wrongheaded. It frequently failed to articulate its decisions adequately and sometimes appeared to doubt the importance of adequate articulation.[110] It was frequently self-righteous and intolerant of competing considerations. At times it flouted the Court conventions when adherence to them would have cost little and might have marshalled greater support for the innovations it was effecting.[111] Strangely enough, one of the most seri-

---

106. F. GRAHAM, THE SELF-INFLICTED WOUND (1970).
107. *Id.* at 15.
108. *Id.* at 184-93; R. HARRIS, THE FEAR OF CRIME 22-29 (1969). Among the other important factors contributing to the temper of the times was undoubtedly the assassination of Robert Kennedy in the spring of 1968.
109. Act of June 19, 1968, Pub. L. No. 90-351, 82 Stat. 197.
110. *Cf.* Hart, *Foreword, The Supreme Court, 1958 Term,* 73 HARV. L. REV. 84 (1959).
111. Thus, in Mapp v. Ohio, 367 U.S. 643 (1961), the Court overruled Wolf v. Colorado, 338 U.S. 25 (1949), even though the latter case was not cited in the appellant's brief. Justice Harlan charged that the majority had "simply 'reached out'" to obtain their result. 367 U.S. at 674.

ous criticisms of the Court is that often, having embarked upon a problem it did not go far enough. This was true not only in *Miranda*. The Warren Court failed to realize its opportunity to place the law of entrapment on a more satisfactory footing and left the way open for the Burger Court to halt promising developments in the Courts of Appeals that might well have led to more reasonable outcomes.[112] Having struggled its way to a new and more useful approach to the fourth amendment in *Katz v. United States*,[113] it failed to pursue the implications of its insight. Sometimes its conflicting motivations appeared paradoxical. In the same period that it was pursuing innovations in the area of pretrial interrogation that many warned were threatening the effectiveness of law enforcement, it stubbornly defended in the name of law enforcement the use of undercover agents and resisted efforts to restrict and regulate their activities.

Much has been made of the Warren Court's "activism." An appraisal involves more than an exercise in the doctrine of the separation of powers. A case does exist for judicial initiative. Within limits the courts can and ought to lead, not simply follow. Recent history demonstrates that judicial action sometimes reflects the aspirations and preferences of the community more accurately than does action of the other branches of government. Federal judges, however, who act within the broad latitudes of "good behavior," are responsible to no political authority. As our history has shown, the federal courts can become obstacles to democratic self-determination, and the resulting consequences can be devastating both to the courts and the country. The Warren Court enjoyed its greatest successes when it advanced solutions that were supported by a broad ethical consensus, as in cases involving the right of impoverished defendants to counsel in the courtroom. When it moved beyond this consensus in the areas of police behavior it was confronted by resistance that was real and seriously constricting. The opposition to *Miranda* represented more than an inflamed and deluded public opinion. The heart of the matter was identified by Justice White when in his dissent he said: "I see nothing wrong or immoral . . . in the police's asking a suspect . . . whether or not he killed his wife . . . ."[114] However incomplete this statement of the underlying ethical issue may be, Justice White's proposition clearly expressed the convictions of a significant fraction of the population.

The central problem of the Warren Court's activism in the criminal area was not that it threatened serious abuses of power by politically irresponsible judges. Rather, it was simply that, despite the Court's

---

112. *See* United States v. Russell, 411 U.S. 423 (1973); Sherman v. United States, 356 U.S. 369 (1958).

113. 389 U.S. 347 (1967); *see* Kitch, *The Supreme Court's Code of Criminal Procedure: 1968-1969 Edition*, 1969 Sup. Ct. Rev. 155.

114. 385 U.S. 436, 538 (1966) (White, J., dissenting opinion).

ingenious, persistent, and, some may feel, heroic efforts to overcome the inherent limitations of judicial power, the Court attempted more than it could possibly achieve. Moreover, the attempt incurred costs. The Court was unable to see the problems of criminal justice in their full complexity. While concentrating on the vindication of individual rights, the Court was unable to offer any contributions to the staggering problems created for the system of criminal justice by the weight of numbers—both numbers of crimes and numbers of persons processed by the system. Indeed, much of what it did exacerbated those problems. This is not to suggest that the Warren Court should have ignored the issues of rights and immunities that confronted it pending administrative housekeeping. Rather, it suggests that until we simultaneously attack the full range of problems afflicting criminal justice, the outcome of our efforts is likely to be partial and unsatisfactory.[115] This, in turn, suggests the necessity of a greater role for legislative and administrative expertise in the approach to these issues.

In the final analysis, the Court will not succeed unless it stimulates a constructive response from the localities and the other branches of government.[116] To a degree frequently overlooked, the Warren Court and those that immediately preceded it produced that response. Legislatures have enacted scores of innovations relating to criminal and juvenile justice. Court rules adopted in the states often responded even more clearly and rapidly to the Court's new directions. Private professional groups like the American Law Institute,[117] the American Bar Association,[118] and the National Commissioners on Uniform State Laws[119] are providing invaluable impetus to legislative reform. The Court has stimulated by far the larger part of this activity. The prospects of a continuing impact of the Warren Court on our institutions depends most importantly on the continuation and enlargement of similar efforts.

Nevertheless, the slowness and perversity of legislative response to the problems of criminal justice are often disheartening. The attitudes revealed by Congress in the Omnibus Crime Control Bill of 1968 are illustrative. One example will suffice. In the closing years of the Warren tenure the Court decided several cases extending the right to counsel to police line-up identification procedures.[120] The Court was wholly right

---

115. *See* Conard, *Macrojustice: A Systematic Approach to Conflict Resolution*, 5 GA. . L. REV. 415 (1971).

116. In some instances the Court explicitly solicited such response. Thus, in Griffin v. Illinois, 351 U.S. 12, 20 (1956), the opinion of Justice Black contained the following language: "The Illinois Supreme Court appears to have broad powers to promulgate rules of procedure and appellate practice. We are confident that the State will provide corrective rules to meet the problem which this case lays bare."

117. ALI, A MODEL CODE OF PRE-ARRAIGNMENT PROCEDURE (Proposed Draft, 1975).

118. ABA, STANDARDS FOR CRIMINAL JUSTICE (1973).

119. UNIFORM RULES OF CRIMINAL PROCEDURE (1974).

120. *See* note 65 *supra*.

in recognizing the problem of misidentification as a central one in the administration of criminal justice. The problem here is ,not that of releasing an obviously guilty defendant because of the system's failure to respect his rights. On the contrary, the problem is one of convicting the innocent. Studies reveal that misidentification may well be the greatest peril confronting the innocent person caught up in the criminal process.[121] Whatever the values of the right to counsel in these procedures—and opinions differ[122]—no one is likely to regard it as a sufficient solution to these problems. Alternative devices, possibly including the removal of identification procedures entirely from the police and placing them in the hands of an expert and neutral administrative agency, are required. Congress' rejection of the Court's solution is not surprising. The fact that it contented itself with simply attempting a legislative repeal of the Court's decision without offering anything to deal with the critical problem the Court had identified is deplorable. Yet this is what occurred.[123]

A new allocation of responsibilities is required. The role of the Court will remain critical. It has shown its capacity to identify and dramatize problems in criminal justice administration; this role is an essential catalyst for reform. The Court will have to make the ultimate decisions on the constitutional validity of the solutions devised. Nevertheless, its role is better adapted to review than to initiation. If categorical rules for the system are needed, it is better that other institutions formulate most rules. This proposition, however, assumes full and intelligent participation in the process by legislatures and other groups. We shall probably not enjoy more favorable prospects for such constructive participation than in the present post-Watergate era. There is ground for optimism. It is high time.

---

121. The legal and scientific literature is extensive. *See* Levine & Tapp, *The Psychology of Criminal Identification: The Gap from Wade to Kirby,* 121 U. PA. L. REV. 1079 (1973); McGowan, *Constitutional Interpretation and Criminal Identification,* 12 WM. & MARY L. REV. 235 (1970). The prevalence of misidentification as a cause for convictions of the innocent has been demonstrated. *See* E. BORCHARD, CONVICTING THE INNOCENT (1932); J. FRANK & B. FRANK, NOT GUILTY (1957).

122. See materials collected in Y. KAMISAR, W. LAFAVE, & J. ISRAEL, MODERN CRIMINAL PROCEDURE 620-22 (4th ed. 1974).

123. *See* 18 U.S.C. § 3502 (1970).

II. Civil Rights in Times of Economic Stress

Jurisprudential and Philosophic Aspects of Racial Discrimination in Employment

CHARLES L. BLACK, JR.

Though the program does not say so, I have to mention that, in the correspondence leading to my having the pleasure of being here tonight, I was asked to address myself in particular to the philosophic and jurisprudential aspects of our general subject. This topic—or, rather, this wide subject—might be thought an invitation to vagueness. I cannot claim that, in trying to get my thoughts together, I have altogether and firmly declined this invitation. I shall have to let you be the judges as to whether I have declined it at all; my hope will have to be that my vaguenesses will engender some more concrete ideas in your minds, and I console myself with the thought that I am to be followed by someone who may explore some of the more concrete legal problems.

I have been asked, I repeat, to talk on the jurisprudential and philosophic aspects of civil rights during periods of economic stress. That is one of those topics that seems quite promising when you are invited, in February, for October. All is not gold that glitters, but there must be a nugget or two, at least, in hills so resplendent. Along about Labor Day, or the autumnal equinox, as days sadly shorten, you begin slowly to realize that, after all, you are not a philosopher in any sense, not intellectually, not temperamentally, and are an expert in jurisprudence only by virtue of a Special Act of the Corporation of Yale University, which Act has recently been repealed by implication, and a new title conferred which does summary justice to the bald truth that you really are just a lawyer, and nothing but that. What I shall do is to take the "jurisprudence and philosophy" part of my subject as an invitation to general thought, without reference, except in far-off sorrow, to clear and present political possibility, or to fine-grained legal doctrine. That is the most I can make of it; I hope I shall not be judged to have given short weight.

I shall limit myself in another quite drastic and even arbitrary way. "Civil rights" has come to be a term of art, referring primarily to the right to be immune from all sorts of racial discrimination, or discrimination on some similarly irrational ground, analogous to race. I do not forget that there are in our society other groups than blacks who are subject to such discrimination, and I hope I shall not fall into the error of supposing, to cite two very important examples, that the problems of Chicanos or of American Indians are just the same as those of blacks. The Indians differ in that many of them remain, in residence or in feeling, more or less tribalized, as well as in ways not so easily pinpointed. The problems of the Chicanos may often contain and be complicated by a language problem, and in subtler shadings may also differ from the problems of black people seeking enjoyment of their civil rights. I have not forgotten, either, that the oldest, the most inveterate and ingrained injustice in all societies is the treatment of about half the population—women—a problem utterly unique. Tonight, however, I shall stay principally or entirely with the problem of black civil rights, partly because that is what I know best, and partly because some, though not all, of my thoughts seem to me applicable to these other fields—though as to this, I stand ready to be not so much corrected as instructed.

I am invited, however, to discuss something more specific than civil rights in general, even black civil rights. The assignment of topic assumes that this subject has special connections with periods of economic stress. It is not hard to see, in general, what this connection is. Most if not all goods of all kinds are always more or less scarce. But this scarcity is perceived and felt most sharply during times of economic difficulty—indeed, that is in a sense the defining character of such a time. And I suppose the question implicitly put by my subject is: "To what extent and in what manner, if at all, ought blacks to be specially treated with respect to the scarcities that pinch at such times?"

I find it quite impossible to disengage this question from the larger one of our obligation to black people at all times. Let me explore with you, by way, I am sure, of review, the source and nature of this obligation.

It is one of the most illuminating facts of history to me, though it can scarcely be to others, that I was taught to play the harmonica by a man who had been born into slavery and raised to middle adolescence as a slave. I received this instruction in the 1920's, when he was about 75 and I was about 10. Figure it out. I don't need to figure it; I remember the Confederate veterans in Austin. I carry this fact around with me, as I usually carry a harmonica of the same sort we used, to remind me that the wrong done to our black fellow-citizens is not a thing of ancient history, its effects dampened by long swirling ages, like the Roman destruction of Carthage, but a thing of historical yesterday, even in its most horrible manifestation. I stand before you, a man who runs a couple of miles a day, who gets by as a law professor in this year of grace 1975, and who can even communicate to some extent with his own adolescent children. Yet I have talked of slavery with an alert man who knew it at first hand, from underneath.

I think it unnecessary to go into detail as to the effects of slavery on black people. The sequel to slavery was such as to preserve rather than to dissipate these effects. The segregation system, aside from all its baneful characteristics as a thing in itself, aside from its all-pervading function of stigmatizing and insulting blacks, day by day and hour by hour, had the further effect of ensuring that the people who had been so disadvantaged by slavery would remain in greatest part one people, self-known and identified by others, so that the chance of any rapid dissipation of the effects of slavery itself was minimal. Instead, the pertinacity of these effects was maximized, while at the same time new wrongs, also disabling, were being perpetrated—the wrong of segregation, a stigma in itself, a ritual of untouchability, and the wrong of virtual ineligibility for most of the good things in life—good jobs, good homes, good education. Of course some blacks broke through; talent and strength of character will once in a while break through any system, and black people have plenty of both. But if there ever was in history a visible chain linking cause and effect, over a rather short period, it is the chain linking our wantonly wicked treatment of black people, during slavery and after slavery, with their difficulties today. We are not talking about conditions under the Fourth Pharasnic Dynasty as they affect Mr. Sadat and his people.

I would like at this time to interpolate what is not so much a digression as a necessary caution. If what we were talking about were a *legal* liability to compensate black people for these wrongs and their effects, the problem of "state action," as it has been called, might enter in. The fourteenth amendment, we were told long ago, protects only against "state action." For quite a long time, with what now is seen as deceptive consistency, this rule of law was uttered but not applied. Quite correctly, I think, the Supreme Court always found the requisite governmental involvement. Recently, there has come down at least one decision[1] so amazingly reactionary on this score that it is hard to believe the Court really would generalize its doctrine. I shall not in this place elaborate on this, because our obligation to black people results, if it exists at all, from the actions of a whole society rather than merely from those of a governmental structure, and white people in overwhelming preponderance have, by their actions and by their acquiescences, during slavery and since slavery, contributed to build the structure of disadvantage and frustration within which black people have had to live. If the

---

1. Jackson v. Metropolitan Edison Co., 419 U.S. 435 (1974).

past can create moral obligations in the present, then it is the obligation of all of us to keep going until the last vestige of past wrong is eliminated, quite without reference to the niceties of the "state action" doctrine.

You may have noted that I have cast several of my assertions in the conditional mode: "if the past can create moral obligations"; "this obligation, if it exists at all. . . ." I think it quite legitimate to query the existence of this obligation, on the part of people now, to treat specially a race disadvantaged because of the action of others in the past, even the recent past. But in the end, of course, moral obligations are never provable, because they always rest on unprovable major premises, hidden or unhidden. After all considerations are canvassed, one must simply make up one's mind, on one's moral rather than on one's intellectual responsibility. All I can do here is to raise a few points which might tend to push the minds of doubters—to remove objections—and then leave the listener to consider.

I think most doubts revolve around the problem of guilt. Many people quite properly resent an attribution of guilt in themselves, inherited from others, when they themselves do not have any consciousness of having wronged black people, or of having contributed to their being at a disadvantage. One form of this objection is sometimes interposed by descendants of relatively recent immigration, who say (and one has both heard and read this):

> My ancestors were not here in the times of slavery, and had nothing to do with the trend of events immediately following slavery. When they came here, the wrong was already done; as recent immigrants, caught in their own struggles, they had no chance to revise what they found. How can I, the descendant of totally innocent people—innocent in the sense that they were not even around when this system was being put in place—be saddled with the guilt of others?

My answer would be that if the American people stand under an obligation generated by American history, then anyone who *joins* the American people, becoming one with and of the American people, has to assume, with the benefits of that total incorporation, whatever obligations rest on the American people. And although it is not logically relevant at the present juncture, it is emotionally necessary to me, as I inwardly call the roll of my companions-at-arms in the racial fight, to add just now that the children of recent immigration have in fact—at least among lawyers—borne a share of the battle overwhelmingly out of proportion to their numbers. Still, the objection as to obligation persists, and I think is entirely answered by the concept of naturalization as the equivalent for all purposes of citizenship by birth—a concept which, so far as it concerns benefits, I have elsewhere stated as radically as it can be stated, opposing every possible form of discrimination, for any purpose, between the two kinds of citizenship which I believe the fourteenth amendment by implication to have made one.

One finds, watered down, much the same sort of thing among Northerners—and here I tread especially warily, for I imagine that in this part of Illinois there are in the audience a good many of what we in ancient Texas would have called Yankees. Here I think the answers are many. Perhaps the most important is that it is simply not true that the North has not directly contributed—massively contributed—to the disadvantaging of the blacks. On one day, the Territorial Legislature of Oregon voted that slavery should not be permitted in that Territory. A noble resolve, That! On the same legislative day, I believe, it was voted that no free blacks at all be admitted to the Territory. If you look at the meagerly reported explanations, you find that these two actions were quite rationally connected in the minds of those who took them. The Territorial Legislature was against slavery on the ground that it was rather feared that emancipation would sooner or later come, and then, if you had allowed slavery, there would be a lot of free blacks hanging about. In other words, the motive behind *both* votes—the seemingly anti-racist and the obviously racist—was the same. No blacks at all were to be allowed in an enormous section of the northern United States. School segregation started in the North, as the *Plessy*[2] Court gleefully stressed. All kinds of discrimination, except slavery, flourished in the North, before, during and long after the Civil War. This has somehow become more visible in relatively recent times. When I was in my salad days, I hung around bars in New York a good deal; I don't recommend such use of one's time, but truth is truth. I remember that, in those times, when a black person was in the bar, and when I spoke a few words and my speech made me manifest as coming from the South, there sometimes was a tension all but visible in the air, and, more than once, common friends had to take upon themselves the duty of a whispered explanation, to the black, that I was really all right. I don't hang around bars much anymore, finding it incompatible with the joint characters of *pater familias* and senior professor, but I do move around a good deal, and can rarely bring myself to keep quiet long enough for it not to become quickly obvious, to black and white alike, that the bear, growling yet of the hole wherein he was born, is of Southern provenance. Yet I now find never a hint of stiffening or tension on the part of blacks, when this fact about my origin comes clear. I think they now know quite well that it was a mistake to see the enemy as located exclusively in places of lower latitude. Of course the southern treatment of blacks has been the more luridly wicked. But in what has been done to the American black, there is quite enough blame to go around, and much of it sticks like pitch to the North.

---

2. Plessy v. Ferguson, 163 U.S. 537 (1896).

Moreover, the historical relation of the North to Southern white racism itself has long been, by deliberate choice, one of relieved acquiescence. I leave aside the Northern tolerance of slavery, for that was doubtless inevitable. But broadly though accurately speaking, I think, it was the North at least as much as the South that made the decision, some dozen years after the Civil War, that the promises of the fourteenth and fifteenth amendments were to be broken.

In this connection, I remind you again that we are not talking about "state action," but about the actions of a whole society. West Point, theoretically, admitted blacks, but their lives were made intolerable by their fellow-cadets. Girard College was for whites only. The racially restrictive covenant was a northern quite as much as southern device. I myself remember that some 30 years ago it was a live question, on which people could actually take sides, whether the Stork Club did right in refusing to serve Josephine Baker. Jackie Robinson had to "break into" baseball—imagine our looking on the grudging tolerance that made that possible as though it were a virtue! Louis Armstrong, on whose death flags were half-masted in Europe, couldn't have gotten into a decent hotel in many northern as well as southern cities, until quite recent times; to cite an intangible—often more destructive of the spirit than tangible things—when Armstrong appeared as a guest-star on Bing Crosby's program, I seem to remember that the script had him say "Mr. Crosby" while Bing said "Louie"—a thing which, in all fairness, I must say probably hacked and embarrassed Crosby, who has never shown a trace of personal racism and who undoubtedly respected the great artist, more than it did anybody else.

The whole people of the United States bear the responsibility for the black past and for what it has meant and means to the black present. And I want to emphasize here still once more that I am not talking about the question of legal liability for reparations. My colleague, Boris Bittker, in a monograph[3] which should be widely read, has explored the latter narrower question, and quite rightly discerns many difficult technical problems, easier (or so I read him as asserting) to raise than to solve. What we have to do with here is something quite different. It is the responsibility of a whole people to take steps to right a great wrong. It is a responsibility not measurable by judicial judgment resting on the law of admeasured remedies, but by the *fact of dissipation of the consequences of that wrong.* It is, for that very reason, a responsibility not for money payment only—though money is abundantly needed—but for specific performance, not to any premeasured degree, but until the crooked is made straight.

As I think over the foregoing, and as I recollect conversations and readings through the years on this subject, I reiterate that the key to

---

3. *See* B. BITTKER, THE CASE FOR BLACK REPARATIONS (1973).

resistance to these ideas, on many levels of intellectualism, and with respect both to the specific points I have made and to the whole idea of national obligation in the premises, is reluctance to admit *guilt.* People who have themselves done nothing wrong, or little wrong, can hardly be brought to feel guilty. To this, let me say that I heartily agree. I do not feel particularly guilty on this subject. I imagine most of you people here are in my position; we haven't done as much as we would like to have done, and should have done, but we have done some things, and we have not knowingly contributed to the wrong. Of such stuff human *guilt* is not made—or at least not the sort of guilt for earthly expiation. But—and this distinction is, I think, absolutely crucial—we are not talking about guilt. We are talking about *responsibility.* Our national society—the only one we have, the only one from which we derive all the *benefits* of national social organization—has so acted as to place millions of black people in a situation of misfortune, and of vulnerability to misfortune, which is beyond honest question unfair and totally inconsonant with our professions of national principle. Our responsibility, which is not guilt and has really nothing to do with guilt, either on our own part or even on that of our forebears, seems to me to arise out of our accepting and keeping membership in the polity that has done this, with all its benefits, and out of the inconsonance between our present professions of principle and our acquiescence in the situation produced by a radical and long-continued breach of principle.

To talk in legal terms, we have been too unimaginative in our choice of analogies. Obligations are not all *ex delicto.* Some may arise by estoppel, for example—and here one thinks of the inerasable words of the Declaration of Independence. Perhaps more to the point, there are obligations *quasi ex contractu*—for work and labor performed, for benefits had and received; that, I believe, was the theory of the Second Inaugural. Other concepts, such as the constructive trust, come to mind.

If you go this far, indeed, I think you are led quite irresistibly even further. Let us imagine a situation—just a contemporary situation—in which, for reasons which I ask you to imagine as not even known, twenty million black people were on the whole decidedly poorer, in virtually every tangible and intangible way, than the white population. Let us suppose, as I have said, that history were somehow blotted out of memory and we were altogether unaware that the American polity had introduced these people's ancestors as slaves, and after slavery was given up had treated them as untouchables. Even so, would we not feel a responsibility to take steps to change this position? I think we would, and if I am right then, in this matter, guilt is nothing, even causation is nothing, and present responsibility is everything. But, lest I be thought to have gone too far, let me make it clear that this is only an imaginary situation. I remind you of the revealing historic fact that I was taught to play the harmonica by a former slave, who had grown to the age of 15 during years when, in at least some slave states, it was unlawful to teach him to read and write. And I remind you that, even as he and I played our harmonicas, he and his children could not in any effective sense participate in politics, that he and they lived, even then, under the threat of lynching, that his grandchildren, and probably even his great-grandchildren, went to segregated and plainly inferior schools—that, in sum, American society as a whole, until day before yesterday, grossly discriminated against these people, in ways not so much likely as certain to place them at a nearly hopeless disadvantage. No one can establish, by logical demonstration, that such a course of events generates a responsibility of corrective action, not discharged until correction is fully effected. All I can say is that if I found a person who denied this responsibility I would be at a loss to guess what that person thinks it takes for history to generate obligation—or, indeed, for anything to generate obligation.

Underneath what I have said, I think you will see a partly hidden premise, or perhaps, rather, a premise so obvious that it need hardly be stated. That premise is that the prime need is now and for a long time has been *affirmative corrective action*—"reparation" in the larger and perhaps etymological sense of *repair*, of actual removal of the consequences of wrong. It is still true that, if we look at the actions of the *society*, forgetting the "state action" concept, there is abundant raw discrimination against blacks—with respect to housing, to schooling, to employment, and to many other matters. But even as to these straight-out remnants of the older evil, correction must now go hand-in-hand with affirmative action. And it is this, I think, that makes "civil rights in a period of economic stress" a special topic, for three reasons.

First, when the country is hurting economically—and this, I believe, is true whether the hurt be depression, or inflation, or that strange mixture of both from which we have lately suffered—there is likely to be a general decline in moral fervor and energy, with respect to such questions as civil rights or effective racial equality. Interest in justice is to most people a luxury, much easier to give up than cigarettes or beer. Just in a general way, it seems to me, a white population worried about its own economic future finds it easy to forget the positions of black people. As Huxley, I believe, said, love drives out fear, but fear drives out love—even the love of justice.

Secondly, effective relief of racial injustice demands the spending of money, on programs of all kinds, such as Head Start. It takes money, gushing money, to dissipate the effects of a tradition coming from the days when it was unlawful to teach black people to read; it takes money to get rid of rats in tenements. Yet in times such as these, with our cities openly talking of bankruptcy, and with the national administration far from enthusiastic as to either the adequate financing of programs in being, or (Heaven forbid!) the initiation of any new programs federally funded, the outlook is indeed bleak. Of course, this is never a question of actual lack of money, but a conception of priorities that looks on the salvation of children's minds, or the creating of decent housing conditions for blacks, as frills, easily postponable till shipping subsidies, interstate highways, and the registration of patents and trademarks are securely provided for. The effect on black people is disastrous, in material ways and in the flickering-out of hope.

As to both these problems, interconnected and perhaps even identical as they are, there is really no jurisprudential or philosophic insight that avails. The inability or unwillingness of the dominant part of America to treat the remedial needs of black people as an emergency, with something near a first-priority call on our resources, in bad times as well as good, is something that falls under the heading of shame rather than under the heading of philosophy. And the shame is the greater because it is likely to be in bad times that black people, the first sufferers from a slackening in economic activity and from inflation, need help the most.

This thought brings me to a third point—one that really does contain dilemmas of moral philosophy and of jurisprudential foundations. Some of the reparative needs of black people cannot be satisfied by public money, whether given directly to them or expended on programs set up to help them. Some of these needs can be satisfied only in kind, and very often the choice must be made between the valid claim of a black to preference by way of restitution for years or centuries of wrong, and the claim of the white man, equally valid in itself, not to be made the scapegoat and singled-out sufferer for wrongs in which he himself had no special part—not on a fair *pro rata* basis, as taxpayer, but by a severe loss falling on himself alone. We have recently seen a clash of this kind, or at least one presented as being of this kind, in the celebrated *De Funis* case.[4] I may say, parenthetically, that I think the Court was supremely wise, as well as technically in the right, in dismissing that case as moot, which it so clearly was, and thus avoiding decision of an issue which may disappear, or come to have much less importance, as time passes and which cannot be decided with any full satisfaction, either as to law or as to morality, in favor of either party. But periods of economic recession present unavoidable issues of a somewhat similar form, for they render scarce not only money but also things not altogether measurable in money. Let us think together a little about what is undoubtedly the most agonizing of these problems—the problem of access to satisfying work.

I state the problem that way because—jurisprudentially and philosophically, if you like—that is its tough and irremediable essence. A

---

4. DeFunis v. Odegaard, 416 U.S. 312 (1974).

man laid off from work, in times of high unemployment and hence of problematic reemployability, is in part compensated by various sorts of relief payments, and there is no reason, other than present political impossibility, why he should not be fully compensated for all his losses, as far as money can go. But modern psychology has shown, as if ancient common wisdom had not, that access to productive work is not compensable with money.

In bad times, the most common rule, hardened into one of the bargained privileges of seniority, has been that of "last in, first out." This was not in itself a bad rule. It had the merit of definiteness, and honored one of the most ancient human feelings, that of prescription. Where it prevailed, it eliminated corrupt favoritism. But consider how it works on blacks. As we have just passed through a period of constantly growing employment of blacks in jobs they never before were allowed to hold, black workers are, except in the lowliest occupations, on the average far junior to their white co-workers. The seemingly neutral and fair "last hired, first fired" rule massively and fairly consistently translates into "blacks fired." And the firing, remember is out into an economy of high unemployment and one containing, in spite of all legal efforts, a very considerable measure of anti-black discrimination in hiring—into a world which, the last time I looked, had an adult black male unemployment rate of around 25 percent. And think of the irony of this to its victims. In very many cases, the black is "last hired" because of rank racial discrimination in the past. He now finds that, in effect, this past wrong, with its inevitable corollary of low seniority, is to result in his being kicked in the teeth yet once again.

On the other hand, the alternative is to fire a white worker of higher seniority. This may be a man who had no part in the prior discrimination, which is traceable not to him but to the employer, or to industry custom, reinforced by the acquiescence or even the preferences of the whole society. Yet the employer, the industry, and the whole society pay nothing; this one white worker bears the whole load on his own shoulders—the economic loss, and those demoralizing effects of unemployment which can be fully appreciated only by those who have either experienced them or seen them at first hand.

I have stated here a genuine dilemma—a case, or class of cases, in which justice cannot be done—in which, instead, wrong must be done. The thought of the possibility of such cases comes hard to the modern mind. The problem *demonstratedly without solution*—a familiar phenomenon in mathematics—offends the generality of people. Lives have been given to trying to calculate π as a rational number, though a very simple demonstration shows this to be impossible. Yet the law faces such problems all the time, and *must* solve them—or, rather, must act as if it had. While airplane engines can be adequately built with π taken to only five or perhaps six places, there come times in life, and in law, when the impossible decision is a necessary decision. We have one of them here.

The law has one technique, often though not always useful, for making such problems more manageable, and that is by reducing their instances, one by one, to minute concreteness, so that the *weight* of competing considerations in the very case may be taken into account, though the arguments on a high level never can meet logically, and the classic techniques of refutation and rebuttal never can avail.

At the risk, then, of leaving the purely jurisprudential and philosophical, let me state you one hypothetical case rather closely similar to a case actually pending.[5] Let us say that a trucking company, on the undisputed evidence, refused as a matter of policy, until late in 1970, to hire black drivers, though some black applicants were clearly qualified, and though, to maintain its lily-white standard, the company hired white drivers deficient in respect of accident record and on-the-road experience. Let us take the case of a single black worker, turned down in 1970 under this policy, but—as a result of severe pressure—finally hired by this same company in 1972. When times get bad, and layoffs start, should this black get the benefit of a seniority dating back to his original rejection, or should all white drivers hired before he was actually taken on get full benefit of their own factual seniority?

It is to be noted here that the original policy of denying employment to blacks was not only wrong but flatly unlawful in 1970, that the same company is involved, that the very man claiming seniority was turned down though qualified; it ought perhaps to be presumed that the white drivers, perceiving the absence of blacks on the work-force, either knew or should have known of the discriminatory policy. The time, moreover, is short—a quite relevant consideration where the principal equity proffered by the white with greater actual seniority is that of action in reliance, both as to taking and as to staying on the job.

For my part, I should have no difficulty in pronouncing in favor of the black worker under these equities. But let us imagine a very different case. The evidence unequivocally establishes that a black, 25 years ago, wanted to work in a certain branch of electrical appliance assembly work. He knew that he had no chance, and so did not even apply—a thoroughly realistic assessment and action in 1950 as to many industries. In 1965, after the passage of the Civil Rights Act of 1964, he applies for and receives the necessary on-the-job training in a company complying with the Act, turns out to possess the requisite aptitudes in good measure, and becomes a very satisfactory worker in just the sort of job he would have held had his aspirations of 1950 been attainable. When times get bad, what should his seniority be for "last-hired-first-fired" purposes?

5. Franks v. Bowman Transp. Co., Inc., 495 F.2d 398 (5th Cir. 1974), *rev'd*, 44 U.S.L.W. 4356 (Mar. 24, 1976) (No. 74-728).

Here many factors are changed. The original discrimination, though cruel and irrational, was not unlawful. The company concerned is only diffusely connected with the original wrong; its white workers hired in 1950 and before would have had to be far ahead of their times, further ahead perhaps than it is realistic or fair to require, to realize that any wrong at all was occurring. Most important of all, the white worker of just under twenty-five years standing has invested not a few months but the better half of a working life in this job. To fire him is to ask him to pay a grievous price, in his own person, for a wrong which was general and societal, while the society as a whole goes scot-free.

I do not know how I would decide such a case. I have no doubt that the black has been wronged, and that the plain consequence of the wrong is his low seniority. But I feel the grim inequity, too, of loading the white with so terrible a consequence of a wrong not at all of his personal doing. And if you, like me, stand doubtful before such a case, I think you will agree that other cases, more extreme, could be stated, wherein the equity of the white worker would rather plainly outweigh that of the black.

In the whole range of these cases, as I have said, we have to do with a general problem, common enough in life but very hard of acceptance to the mind oriented not only toward problem-solving but toward the assumption of universal problem-solubility. We are faced with situation after situation in which justice is unattainable, in which definite wrong must be done to someone. No solution of such a problem produces any feeling of satisfaction. Yet action must and will be taken, one way or the other.

I would hope that there might come into being some recognition of the fact that such problems, calling for the weighing of competing equities rather than the discovery, by reasoning, of the location of justice, call in many cases for legislative rather than whole-cloth judicial solution. Courts are not always well-equipped to choose between two plain wrongs. The courts have to struggle along and do the best they can, if Congress gives no help. But I would hope that Congress, combining its commerce power and its power under section 5 of the fourteenth amendment, would attempt to assist the courts at least by the establishment of some guidelines. Perhaps administrative agencies might also have some part to play here as well.

Now to go back: when it comes to the diminishing or extinction of programs involving allocation of general public resources to the helping of black people in hard times, there is no justice problem, really. Very plainly, what we should be doing is augmenting rather than diminishing such aid, for the need is the greater. When the problem is access to something which, like productive work or educational opportunity, cannot wholly be created by money, then the terrible crux I have been discussing arises.

The thing nearest a solution to this problem lies, of course, in its *transcendence*, by the creation of a society which accepts and discharges, as to *all*, the responsibility of the *real social contract*—the quasi-contract, if you like—which in my view imposes on all of us the obligation to see that, in return for their living at peace within the society, *all* people, black and white, share in the good things of life. But here, perhaps, I leave my assigned subject, for a broader one to which, in my mind, it irresistibly leads. I can only speak my sorrow, which I am sure many of you share, that there are no signs at all that movement toward this goal impends—and my fear for the future of a society that so flagrantly and with such insouciance refuses to move toward fulfilling an obligation that seems so plain.

Race Discrimination in Employment:
What Price Equality?

HARRY T. EDWARDS

Herein lie buried many things which if read with patience may
show the strange meaning of being black here at the dawning of
the Twentieth Century. The meaning is not without interest to
you, Gentle Reader; for the problem of the Twentieth Century is
the problem of the color line. [W. E. B. Du Bois, *The Souls of
Black Folk* (1904)]

I. INTRODUCTION

The story of race discrimination in America is an old tale that
seemingly knows no end. The promise of the Emancipation Proclamation—the hope for true freedom and real equality—has yet to see the
full light of day in Black America. Blacks still suffer in America
because they are black; they are still denied decent housing, equal
education and fair employment. Blacks no longer live in slavery, but
they still live in what W. E. B. Du Bois once called a "caste system,"
"founded on color discrimination, peonage, intimidation and mob-vio-
lence."[1] This paper will consider one facet of this caste system, namely,
race discrimination in employment.

The current recession has raised some serious issues about the
declining status of blacks in the job market and it has caused many
persons to consider the implementation of special remedial measures to

*Much of the research for this lecture was done when the author was
preparing an article dealing with the more narrow subject of* Preferential
Remedies for Employment Discrimination *in* 74 MICH. L. REV. 1 (1975).
*Because of an overlap in the subjects covered by this lecture and the article
dealing with preferential remedies, certain portions of the text of both are
the same. The author wishes to acknowledge and express his gratitude for
the research assistance given him by Ms. Susan Mentser, B.A., 1975, Swarth-
more College.*

1. Du Bois, *Three Centuries of Discrimination*, in 54 THE CRISIS 362 (1947).

protect blacks against job loss. Outlining the issues associated with employment discrimination in current economic and legal terms would be a simple enough task; but the current situation does not tell the whole story. The problem of race discrimination in employment is significant because it has been with us for so long. The problem has defied many remedial efforts and caused great suffering for many black persons.

Race discrimination in employment today takes on a special meaning when viewed from a historical perspective. Only when we consider the problem in this vein may we fairly appraise some of the current legal debates over appropriate remedies for job bias. As will be hereinafter shówn, the pattern of race discrimination in employment has been so pervasive for so long in this country that extreme measures may be necessary to cure the problem.

II.   THE HISTORY OF RACE DISCRIMINATION IN EMPLOYMENT: A SHORT SUMMARY OF A LONG STORY

In 1939, approximately 75 years after the Civil War, the median annual income from wages and salaries for black families and individuals was merely $489, or 37 percent of the corresponding median annual income for whites.[2]   By 1952, the median annual income for blacks and other minorities had risen to 57 percent of that of whites. However, no further improvement was seen in the black-white income gap until 1966, when the ratio finally reached 60 percent.[3]

In an article considering the status of American nonwhites between 1940 and 1960, Norval D. Glenn states that most of the improvement in the relative economic standing of nonwhites was made before 1949. The demand for black labor during World War II contributed greatly to the overall improvement in nonwhite income as did the concomitant rural to urban shift. In 1950, 64.3 percent of the white population and 61.7 percent of the nonwhite population were living in urban areas. However, by 1960, the figure for nonwhites had risen by nearly 11 percent to 72.4 percent, while the figure for whites had risen by only 5 percent to 69.5 percent.[4]   Viewing the recent economic patterns of American nonwhites, Glenn says:

The relative economic standing of nonwhite families went up moderately during the Korean conflict but declined during the late 1950's to about the level of the late 1940's. This fluctuation and the marked nonwhite gains during the early 1940's make it appear

---

2.   C. Killingsworth, *Jobs and Income for Negroes* 13, Policy Papers in Human Resources and Industrial Relations, No. 6 (1968) [hereinafter cited as Killingsworth].

3.   U.S. Bureau of the Census, *The Social and Economic Status of the Black Population in the United States,* 1974, at 25, Series P-23 No. 54 (1975) [hereinafter cited as Census Bureau].

4.   Glenn, *Some Changes in the Relative Status of American Nonwhites, 1940 to 1960,* 24 PHYLON 109, 117-18 (1963) [hereinafter cited as Glenn].

that the relative economic status of nonwhites goes up during periods of prosperity and full employment induced by national emer-
gencies, and levels off or declines during recessions or periods of
relatively slow economic expansion.[5]

Between 1947 and 1962, the average income of blacks increased
by 106 percent, from $1,600 to $3,300, compared with a 98 percent
increase for whites, from $3,200 to $6,200. However, the absolute
dollar growth was much greater for whites. From 1947 to 1955,
income level rose faster for blacks than for whites; but from 1955 to
1962, the reverse was true.[6] During the 1960's, gains in black income
relative to that of whites were substantial. The gain between 1965 and
1969 was greater than that in the entire period from 1947 to 1965.
However, the black median income in 1969 ($6,169) was still lower
than that of whites in 1959 ($7,106). The absolute dollar gap between
the races remained constant at about $3,500 throughout the 1960's.[7]

The income distributions of blacks and whites have gained some
similarity in recent years. In 1963, the largest percentage of black
workers were concentrated in the $2,000 to $2,999 category (17.6
percent), while for whites the largest percentage (15.6 percent) earned
between $10,000 and $14,999. In 1972, the largest percentages of
both blacks and whites were in the $15,000 to $24,999 category (14
percent for blacks as compared to 25.6 percent for whites).[8]

Black families with both a husband and wife present and families
with heads under 35 years of age have consistently earned a higher
percentage of income than the average black family.[9] However, it is
noteworthy that, since the late 1950's gains in income made by black
women relative to white women have been more substantial than those
made by black men. Between 1959 and 1969, median incomes rose 60
percent for black women, but only 35 percent for black men. Whereas
income at the same educational level for black and white females has
grown nearly equal, there have been greater and more pervasive inequities in the income distribution among black men. As late as 1969,
black men who had completed 4 years of college were earning less than
white males who had only completed high school.[10]

Blacks in the South have consistently lagged behind those in other
areas of the country in terms of economic advancement. In 1959, of

---

5. *Id.* at 118.
6. Henderson, *Regions, Race, and Jobs*, in EMPLOYMENT, RACE AND POVERTY 87
(A. Ross & H. Hill ed. 1967) [hereinafter cited as Henderson].
7. Farley & Hermalin, *The 1960's: A Decade of Progress for Blacks?*, in RACIAL
DISCRIMINATION IN THE UNITED STATES 250 (T. Pettigrew ed. 1975) [hereinafter cited
as Farley & Hermalin].
8. U.S. BUREAU OF LABOR STATISTICS, DEP'T OF LABOR, BULL. NO. 1825, HAND-
BOOK OF LABOR STATISTICS 425, 433 (1974) [hereinafter cited as LABOR STATISTICS].
9. Census Bureau, *supra* note 3, at 37.
10. Farley & Hermalin, *supra* note 7, at 257-61.

the 2.06 million black families with incomes under $3,000,[11] almost three-fourths lived in the South.[12] The North Central region, which had had the highest nonwhite median income in 1949, was surpassed by the Northeast and West in the median income in 1959. During the 1950's, increases in the black-white median income ratio occurred only in the Northeast and West.[13]

According to the Economic Report of the President for 1964, almost two-thirds of nonwhites lived in poverty in 1947, while by 1962, the proportion had dropped to 44 percent.[14] However, the nonwhite population had increased so rapidly during this same period that the actual number of poor blacks in 1962 was only 3 percent less than in 1947, while there was a 27 percent decline in the number of white families living in poverty during the same period.[15] Between 1959 and 1966, the total number of white people in the United States living in poverty declined from 28 million to 20 million, while the number of blacks living in poverty decreased from eleven million to ten million.[16] There were further decreases in the number of black persons and families below the low-income[17] level as the decade of the Sixties progressed.[18] In 1959, 48.1 percent of all black families and 14.8 percent of all white families were below the low-income level.[19] By 1974, these figures had decreased to 27.8 percent and 7 percent respectively.[20]

While these relative income and poverty level income figures do reflect some improvement in the economic status of blacks during the past two decades, the figures are somewhat misleading. In point of

---

11. $3,000 (in prices) for a family of four was established as the poverty line, "the minimum necessary to meet basic needs in contemporary society." The level was set by the Council of Economic Advisers, Economic Report of the President, January 1964, at 57-58, in Killingsworth, *supra* note 2, at 14.

12. Brimmer, *The Negro in the National Economy*, in THE AMERICAN NEGRO REFERENCE BOOK 263 (J. Davis ed. 1966).

13. Glenn, *supra* note 4, at 118.

14. Killingsworth, *supra* note 2, at 14.

15. Henderson, *supra* note 6, at 86-87.

16. Killingsworth, *supra* note 2, at 15.

17. The low-income threshold for a nonfarm family of four was $5,038 in 1974, $4,540 in 1973, and $2,973 in 1959. Families and unrelated individuals are classified as being above or below the low-income threshold using the poverty index adopted by a Federal Interagency Committee in 1969. This index centers around the Department of Agriculture's Economy Food Plan and reflects the differing consumption requirements of families based on their size and composition, sex and age of the family head, and farm-nonfarm residence. The low-income cutoffs for farm families have been set at 85 percent of the nonfarm levels. These cutoffs are updated every year to reflect the changes in the Consumer Price Index. The low-income data exclude inmates of institutions, members of the Armed Forces living in barracks, and unrelated individuals under 14 years of age. For a more detailed explanation, see Current Population Reports, Series P-60, No. 98; Census Bureau, *supra* note 3, at 42.

18. Census Bureau, *supra* note 3, at 42-43.

19. *Id.* at 43.

20. *Id.*

fact, extraordinary racial inequalities still exist in the job market. Blacks have always suffered the worst effects from unemployment and they have always been relegated to the lowest paying, least significant jobs in American society; these two factors alone have always appeared to substantially nullify the modest gains made by blacks in relative income.

Blacks have generally had higher rates of unemployment than whites according to figures going back as far as the 1930's. The 1937 Unemployment Census stated 26 percent of black males were unemployed as compared with 18 percent of white males. For females, the rates were 32 percent and 24 percent respectively.[21] Maurice Davie, in *Negroes in American Society,* explained that "[b]ecause of their higher rate of unemployment and because of their smaller resources, proportionally more Negroes than whites were on relief during the depression period of the 1930's."[22] In 1935, approximately one-fourth of blacks were on relief as compared with less than one-seventh of whites. The figures for cities, where unemployment was greater, were 39 percent of blacks on relief and 14 percent of whites.[23]

In 1940, blacks continued to suffer higher levels of unemployment than whites. In Philadelphia, one-third of black males, not counting those on work relief projects, were registered as unemployed. In New York and St. Louis, the corresponding proportion was one-fifth. Females also had higher unemployment rates in several of the larger Northern cities. For the 14 to 19 year age group in urban areas, the 1940 Census reported that 36 percent of nonwhite males and 29 percent of white females were jobless.[24]

The largest black-white differentials for unemployment were in the North Central region and the lowest, for men, were in the South. The nonwhite unemployment rate was also lower in the South than it was in the rest of the country. However, since blacks were overrepresented in agriculture in the South, the low unemployment rate probably belied a certain degree of under-employment.[25] A higher incidence of part-time work and part-time unemployment was also much more common to blacks than whites.[26] Arthur M. Ross estimated that

between 1956 and 1961 the percentage of employed Negroes in nonagricultural industries working part time . . . was never lower than 18 percent, whereas it averaged about 13 percent for white

21. M. DAVIE, NEGROES IN AMERICAN SOCIETY 110 (1949) [hereinafter cited as DAVIE].

22. *Id.*

23. *Id.*

24. G. MYRDAL, AN AMERICAN DILEMMA 302 (1944) [hereinafter cited as MYRDAL].

25. Killingsworth, *Negroes in a Changing Labor Market,* in EMPLOYMENT, RACE, AND POVERTY 61-62 (A. Ross & H. Hill ed. 1967) [hereinafter cited as Killingsworth in EMPLOYMENT].

26. Ross, *The Negro in the American Economy,* in EMPLOYMENT, RACE, AND POVERTY 28-29 (A. Ross & H. Hill ed. 1967) [hereinafter cited as Ross in EMPLOYMENT].

males. The incidence of part-time work was more common among Negro females also.[27]

Rashi Fein, in his "Economic and Social Profile of the Negro American," summarized the black worker's situation as follows: "The Negro faces higher unemployment rates, more frequent periods of unemployment in a given year, longer duration of unemployment, more part-time rather than full-time work—and all this is true even when occupation is held constant."[28] In 1948, the unemployment rate for blacks and other minorities was 5.9 percent as compared with 3.5 percent for whites. In 1950, the unemployment rate rose to 9 percent for blacks and other minorities, then fell to 4.5 percent in 1953. But, in 1954, it jumped to 9.9 percent and since then has generally been about twice the white unemployment rate.[29]

Whites enjoyed a longer period of postwar prosperity, with unemployment rates under 6 percent until 1958.[30] Unemployment peaked for blacks and other minorities at 12.4 percent in 1961 and then gradually declined to 6.4 percent in 1969. There was another rise to 10 percent in 1972. The unemployment rate for black females has been somewhat higher than that of males since 1962. Unemployment rates have been highest for males and females in the 16 to 19 year old age group, and progressively lower at higher ages, with the exception of the 65 year old and older age group.[31]   During the first half of the 20th century, blacks underwent a general shift from agricultural to nonagricultural occupations. From 1890 to 1910, black male workers employed in the South in nonagricultural occupations increased by two-thirds, or more than 400,000. The increase was due mainly to growth in the number of "Negro jobs," those jobs which were most unpleasant or dangerous, such as sawing and planing mills, coal mining, and maintenance work on railroads. From 1910 to 1930, however, the number of Negro males engaged in nonagricultural work in the South increased by less than one-third.[32] Lack of industrial expansion in the South and exclusion from the few industries such as textiles, which did expand, contributed to black unemployment problems.[33] The increase of white women in industry also adversely affected black employment, for black men were not permitted to work with white women under the Southern code. Moreover, as more jobs became mechanized and hence less strenuous or dirty, they were taken over by whites.[34]

---

27. *Id.* at 28.
28. Fein, *An Economic and Social Profile of the Negro American*, 94 DAEDALUS 829 (1965).
29. LABOR STATISTICS, *supra* note 8, at 144.
30. Ross in EMPLOYMENT, *supra* note 26, at 30.
31. LABOR STATISTICS, *supra* note 8, at 144, 151-53.
32. A. ROSE, THE NEGRO IN AMERICA 102-03 (1944) [hereinafter cited as ROSE].
33. Killingsworth, *supra* note 2, at 10-11.
34. ROSE, *supra* note 32, at 102-03.

Between 1910 and 1930, the number of male black workers in nonagricultural pursuits in the North more than doubled, increasing by 480,000.[35] Gunnar Myrdal, in *An American Dilemma*, cites a variety of factors contributing to black gains in the North, including the scarcity of labor during World War I, the economic boom of the 1920's, the decline in immigration of foreign workers, and the use of blacks by employers to prevent unionization or break strikes.[36] In the 1920's, blacks gained entrance into the automobile and steel industries.[37] The number of black male workers in the building industry, among longshoreman, in garages and in coal mines also grew, as did the number in clothing industries and some food industries such as slaughter and meatpacking houses. Large employment gains for Negroes came chiefly between World War I and the end of the Twenties. In the 1930's job opportunities severely declined, caused partly by the Depression, by discrimination in labor unions and among employers, and by the increasing number of blacks coming North and competing for jobs.[38] Between 1930 and 1940, the total number of blacks employed also declined.[39]

World War II brought about substantial changes in black occupational trends. Labor force shortages brought on by the war caused increased numbers of blacks to obtain jobs. Between 1940 and 1944, the number of blacks in civilian jobs increased by nearly one million. Blacks moved chiefly from agriculture and domestic services into semiskilled and skilled positions in industry.[40] As whites moved into higher paying defense employment, blacks took over the jobs in consumer and service industries.[41] However, blacks made few gains outside of the manual field. Although they maintained the gains they had made during the war, they continued to be severely underrepresented in white collar occupations.[42] In the 1950's there was less improvement in the level of black occupations, and it came more slowly.[43]

Between 1940 and 1960, the largest improvement for blacks occurred in intermediate-level occupations, such as clerical workers, craftsmen, foremen and operatives. Within each occupational group, blacks were concentrated in the lower paying and lower prestige occupations. In addition, they generally earned less than whites in the same occupa-

---

35. *Id.* at 104.
36. MYRDAL, *supra* note 24, at 293.
37. Killingsworth, *supra* note 2, at 11.
38. ROSE, *supra* note 32, at 102-03.
39. Ginzberg & Hiestand, *Employment Patterns of Negro Men and Women*, in THE AMERICAN NEGRO REFERENCE BOOK 221 (J. Davis ed. 1966) [hereinafter cited as Ginzberg & Hiestand].
40. Ross in EMPLOYMENT, *supra* note 26, at 17.
41. Weaver, *Negro Labor Since 1929*, in RACE, PREJUDICE AND DISCRIMINATION 122-24 (A. Rose ed. 1951).
42. Ross in EMPLOYMENT, *supra* note 26, at 17.
43. Killingsworth, *supra* note 2, at 11-12.

tions.[44]   Increases in the proportions of blacks in positions as managers and proprietors was slow, due to the poor growth of black small business and the inability of blacks to enter the managerial levels of large corporate and government bureaucracies.[45]

There were only slight increases in the proportion of black men in top level occupations between 1940 and 1960.   Lack of progress in the professional and technical category for black men may be attributed in part to a large decrease in the number of black clergymen, from 17,102 in 1940 to 13,955 in 1960.[46]   In 1940, there were seven times as many white as black men in white collar work; in 1960, there were still three times as many.[47]   In 1960, only 11.4 percent of the employed black male professional, technical and kindred workers were architects, dentists, engineers, lawyers, judges, physicians, or surgeons, in comparison with 31.4 percent of white male professionals who held these positions. For blacks, the largest gains at this level were in lower paying semiprofessional occupations such as welfare and recreation workers and medical and dental technicians.[48]   Black males were overrepresented as operatives, where they had formerly been underrepresented, and continued to be overrepresented among laborers and service workers.[49]

In 1960, the largest proportions of black women were private household workers (36.9 percent) or service workers (22.8 percent), while the largest proportion of white women (32.6 percent) were engaged in clerical and kindred occupations.   The percentage of black women who were private household workers or farm laborers declined substantially from 1940, while the proportion employed as clerical workers rose from 1 percent to 8.9 percent.   There were slight increases for black women in the professional and managerial categories.[50]   The trend toward equality between blacks and whites in the white collar sector was somewhat stronger among women than among men.[51]

III.   THE CURRENT ECONOMIC STATUS OF BLACKS IN THE JOB MARKET

The most recent reports issued by the Bureau of the Census and the Bureau of Labor Statistics indicate that blacks still fall disproportionately low on the scales of income and occupational status, and that they still suffer the worst effects from unemployment.   What is worse is

44.   Broom & Glenn, The Occupations and Income of Black Americans, in BLACKS IN THE UNITED STATES 24-27 (N. Glenn & C. Bonjean eds. 1969) [hereinafter cited as Broom & Glenn].
45.   Glenn, supra note 4, at 111.
46.   Broom & Glenn, supra note 44, at 25-26.
47.   Ginzberg & Hiestand, supra note 39, at 222.
48.   Broom & Glenn, supra note 44, at 26-27.
49.   Ginzberg & Hiestand, supra note 39, at 222-24.
50.   L. LOMAX, THE NEGRO REVOLT 257 (1962).
51.   Ginzberg & Hiestand, supra note 39, at 224.

that the 1973-75 recession has exacerbated the traditional difficulties faced by blacks in the labor market. The National Urban League terms the current economic period "a depression of profound dimensions" for the black community, still suffering the effects of the 1969-71 recession.[52]

The overall income gap between black and white families, as measured by the median income ratio, has widened in the 1970's. The median black family income was only 58 percent of white income in 1974, $7,808 for blacks in comparison to $13,356 for whites. The median income ratio of black to white families showed no change from 1973. After a rise in the 1960's from the 0.54 median income ratio of 1965, there has been a general decline from the 1970 ratio of 0.61.[53]

The Bureau of the Census suggested that "social and economic forces, such as changing attitudes, inflationary pressures, economic slowdown in 1969-70, and the economic recession in 1974," have all played a part in the decline in the median income ratio of black to white families.[54] In addition, it cited "differential changes in the proportion of black and white multiple earner families and work experience patterns of family members among the more important factors contributing to the decreases," attributing variation in these two factors to "changes in (1) family composition, such as the proportion of husband-wife families with wives in the paid labor force and (2) the proportion of families headed by women."[55]

Between 1970 and 1974, the proportion of all black families with wives in the paid labor force declined from 36 to 33 percent, while the white family figure increased from 34 to 37 percent.[56] The Bureau of the Census attributed changes in the proportion of all families with working wives to "first, the proportion of all families which are husband-wife families and, second, the proportion of husband-wife families who have working wives."[57] The proportion of all black families which are husband-wife families declined from 68.1 percent in 1970 to 60.9 percent in 1975, while the proportion of white families which are husband-wife families remained virtually the same, declining only incrementally over the same period.[58] Although the proportion of black husband-wife families with wives in the paid labor force has fluctuated, the 1974 proportion of 54 percent was the same as that in 1970. For the same period, the proportion of white husband-wife families with working wives increased from 38 to 42 percent.[59]

---

52. National Urban League Research Dep't, *Black Families in the 1974-75 Depression* 1 (1975) [hereinafter cited as National Urban League, *Families*].
53. Census Bureau, *supra* note 3, at 24-25.
54. *Id.* at 30.
55. *Id.*
56. *Id.* at 30, 32.
57. *Id.* at 30.
58. *Id.* at 30, 107.
59. *Id.* at 30, 32.

Although the overall median income ratio of black to white families declined between 1970 and 1974, there was no statistically significant change in the black-white median income ratio among families headed by women or families headed by men. The Bureau of the Census attributed this paradox to changes in the proportions of black and white families headed by males and females and in the income received by these families.[60]   The proportion of black families headed by women rose from 28.3 percent in 1970 to 35.3 percent in 1975. The proportion of white families headed by women rose only slightly from 9.1 percent to 10.5 percent for the same period.[61]   Black families headed by women had a substantially lower median income than black families headed by men, $4,465 as compared with $10,365 in 1974. Black families in which the wife was in the paid labor force had an even higher median income in 1974 of $12,982.   Whereas the black-white median income ratio in 1974 was 0.61 for black female-headed families, it was 0.74 for black male-headed families, 0.75 for black husband-wife families, and 0.77 for black husband-wife families in which the wife worked.[62]

Between 1970 and 1974, the percentage of black families with two or more earners fell from 55 to 48 percent, while among whites it remained a fairly level 54 percent with only a slight decline to 53 percent in 1971 and 1972. Traditionally, black multiple earner families, serving as a springboard to economic improvement, have outnumbered those of whites.[63]   There were also reductions in the proportion of black family heads with work experience.   The proportion of black families with a head who worked the previous year declined from 78 to 73 percent between 1970 and 1974.   There was a relatively smaller decline for white counterparts, from 84 to 82 percent.   These factors also contributed to the decline in the black-white median income ratio for families.[64]

The black-white median income ratio for families was also affected by the age of earners and the geographical region in which they lived. In 1973, young[65] black families in which both husbands and wives were present earned 88 percent of the corresponding white family income, a higher percentage of white income than the 74 percent earned by the overall black husband-wife family population.   The black-white median income ratio was an even higher 0.92 for young black families in which both husbands and wives worked.[66]   In the North and West, between

---

60. *Id.* at 30-31.
61. *Id.* at 107.
62. *Id.* at 33.
63. *Id.* at 31, 34.
64. *Id.* at 31.
65. "Young families" refer to those with heads under 35 years of age. *See* Census Bureau, *supra* note 3, at 36.
66. *Id.* at 37-38.

1970 and 1973, young black families in which both husbands and wives worked attained an income level similar to that of whites. In the South, the income gap between blacks and whites narrowed during the same period for young families in which both spouses worked.[67] Thus, the earnings of black wives caused the income gap between blacks and whites to narrow among young husband-wife families. In the South, young black wives had earnings equal to young white wives whereas young black husbands in the South earned only 80 percent of their white counterparts. In the United States as a whole, the earnings of black wives, regardless of age, accounted for a greater percentage of the family income than the earnings of white wives.[68]

In *Black Families in the 1974-75 Depression*, the National Urban League states that ". . . the depression of 1974-75 will substantially erode the economic gains of blacks during the 1960's."[69] Though the 1974 median income for black families increased by 7.4 percent over the 1973 median, adjustments for inflation showed that the median income had actually declined over the past year by 3.2 percent. A similar decrease was noted for whites.[70] Nineteen percent of the 5.5 million black families in the population in March, 1975, had an income of $15,000 or above in 1974 as compared with 42 percent of white families. Thirty-eight percent of black families had incomes of $10,000 or over in 1974 as compared with 68 percent of their white counterparts. Whereas an astounding 23 percent of black families had incomes under $4,000, only 7 percent of white families were under that income level.[71] In real dollars, these proportions, as well as the median income levels, remained essentially the same as the corresponding 1970 figures.[72]

In 1974, 31 percent of the black population, or 7.5 million persons, were below the low-income level. This figure was more than three times the 9 percent proportion of the white population in the same category. Moreover, the proportion of blacks below the low-income level seems to have increased during the 15 years from 1959 to 1973: in 1959, about one-quarter of all persons below the low-income level were black, while in 1973 blacks made up approximately one-third of this group.[73] There were also approximately 164,000 more black families below the low-income level in 1974 than in 1969, bringing the total to 1,530,000 in 1974.[74]

The National Urban League Research Department, in *Black Families in the 1974-75 Depression*, has estimated that in 1973, 44 percent

---

67. *Id.* at 36, 38.
68. *Id.* at 36, 40.
69. National Urban League, *Families, supra* note 52, at 15.
70. Census Bureau, *supra* note 3, at 24.
71. *Id.* at 24, 27.
72. *Id.* at 24.
73. *Id.* at 42.
74. *Id.* at 41-43.

of all black families constituted the " 'actual' or unofficial poor," defined as those earning up to 50 percent above the official low-income level. The National Urban League also calculated that 70 percent of black families headed by women were among the "unofficial" poor in 1973, terming this a reflection of sharply declining job opportunities for black wives and female family heads since 1969.

Fifty-seven percent of black families below the 1973 official low-income level received public assistance. However, for black families below the 1973 low-income level, only one out of four of those headed by men received public assistance, as compared with three out of four of those headed by women.[75] Whereas public assistance was the chief source of unearned income for black families below the 1973 low-income level, public assistance and Social Security were the major sources of unearned income for white counterparts.[76] Approximately 1.4 million, or 40 percent, of households purchasing food stamps were black.[77]

In 1972 and 1973, there were substantial improvements in employment for whites and blacks, followed by large increases in unemployment and cutbacks in employment during 1974 and early 1975 as conditions in the economy worsened. During the third and fourth quarters of 1973, unemployment for both blacks and whites declined to 3½-year lows, falling to 8.6 percent and 4.3 percent (seasonally adjusted), respectively, during the fourth quarter of 1973. Jobless rates began to rise steeply in late 1974, reaching 13.7 percent for blacks and other minorities and 7.6 percent for whites in the first quarter of 1975. The Bureau of the Census reported in 1975 that there have generally been two black workers unemployed for every white worker since the Korean War period except for a decrease in 1970 and 1971.[78] The Bureau of Labor Statistics stated that the unemployment rate for blacks was 13 percent in July, 1975, constituting 1,365,000 unemployed blacks, as compared with 7.9 percent of the white population, or 6,-511,000 whites.[79] The Bureau of the Census reported that the number of "hidden unemployed," those who want jobs but do not look for work because they believe the search would be fruitless, increased sharply. Among those not in the labor force in early 1975, 4.4 percent of blacks and other minorities and 1.6 percent of whites constituted the "hidden unemployed."[80]

The National Urban League developed a different "Hidden Unemployment Index," which included part-time workers seeking full-time

75. Id. at 48.
76. Id. at 41, 48.
77. Id. at 24, 29.
78. Id. at 52-56.
79. Bureau of Labor Statistics, Current Labor Studies, 98 MONTHLY LABOR REVIEW 80 (Sept., 1975).
80. Census Bureau, supra note 3, at 52, 54.

work and those so discouraged that they were no longer actively seeking work.[81]   On this basis the National Urban League reported black "unofficial" unemployment at 25.8 percent in the first quarter of 1975, 26.1 percent in the second quarter.[82]   This constituted a "depression-level" rate of one out of four workers.[83]   White "unofficial" unemployment was 14.7 percent in the first quarter of 1975, 14.2 percent in the second quarter.[84]

The Bureau of the Census reported that the unemployment rate for men of black and other minorities 20 years old or older was 11.1 percent in the first quarter of 1975, and 5.8 percent for white counter-parts, a doubling of the rates for both groups from late 1973.   In the first quarter of 1975, the rate for black women 20 years old or older was 11 percent, nearly equal to that of men in the same period.   For black teenagers, those 16 to 19 years of age, the jobless rate reached 39.8 percent in the first quarter of 1975, compared with 18 percent for white counterparts.[85]   The National Urban League warned that many teenagers ". . . were reaching adulthood without getting the work experience necessary for successful occupational attainment later in life."[86]

The National Urban League Research Department recorded the following additional information about black unemployment.   Among unemployed black men, four out of five had been laid off in the second quarter of 1975 as compared with one-half of the unemployed black women, one-fourth of black teenage males and 13 percent of black teenage females.[87]   The disproportionate impact of the depression on black men was reflected in the increasing unemployment of black men with wives who have traditionally had the lowest unemployment rate among black workers.   About one half of the black men unemployed during the second quarter of 1974 were among the long-term unemployed—out of work for 3 months or more.   While adult black men were likely to be laid off their jobs due to the 1974-75 recession, adult black women were more likely to drop or stay out of the labor force due to unpromising job prospects.   In addition to the unavailability of child care facilities mentioned by the Bureau of Census, the Urban League listed the poor health condition of a rising number of women and traditional race and sex barriers as contributing to the decline in the female work experience.   The Urban League also stated that many

---

81.   A Hidden Unemployment Index was developed by the National Urban League based partly on a formula developed by the Joint Economic Committee of Congress. National Urban League Research Department, *Quarterly Economic Report on the Black Worker* 1 (July, 1975) [hereinafter cited as National Urban League, *Economic Report*].
82.   *Id.* at 5.
83.   *Id.* at 1.
84.   *Id.* at 5.
85.   Census Bureau, *supra* note 3, at 52-53.
86.   National Urban League, *Families, supra* note 52, at 5.
87.   National Urban League, *Economic Report, supra* note 81, at 2.

manpower analysts have estimated black teenage unemployment in the poverty areas of inner cities to be 65 percent or more.[88]

The Urban League has estimated that the problem for blacks has been further compounded by the fact that blacks were less likely to receive unemployment compensation than unemployed whites. Several reasons were cited to explain this phenomenon: the jobs held by blacks were less likely to be covered; blacks were less likely to accumulate a sufficient number of continuous work weeks to establish eligibility; and blacks were more likely to fall into the ineligible categories of new entrants, reentrants and job leavers.[89]

In 1974, unemployment rates were higher for blacks than for whites in all major occupational groups. Black managers and administrators, except those on farms, had the lowest unemployment rate of 3.3 percent. Jobless rates among black salesworkers, nonfarm laborers, and operatives except in transport were above 10 percent.[90] Unemployment rates were highest in industries in which unemployment has traditionally been severe.[91] The highest unemployment rates for black men were in construction (16.5 percent), motor vehicle and equipment industries (16.3 percent) and food and kindred products industries (14.3 percent). They were lowest for railroad and railway express employees (3.6 percent). Among black women, unemployment rates reached highs of 18.1 percent in food and kindred product industries, 15 percent in wholesale and retail trade, and 14.2 percent in other nondurable goods industries. Jobless rates were lowest (3.7 percent) for women in communication and other public utilities. Unemployment rates were also higher for blacks than whites in most major industry groups. In food and kindred products industries, 14.3 percent of black males were unemployed as compared with 4.8 percent of white males; in wholesale and retail trade, 15 percent of black women were jobless in comparison to 7.3 percent of white women.[92]

In an article published in *Blacks in the United States* in 1969, Norval D. Glenn analyzed black employment problems as follows:

> No doubt there is still some tendency for blacks to be the "last hired and first fired," but much of the difference in the unemployment rates of blacks and whites would remain even if there were no discrimination in hiring and firing. Blacks are concentrated in the kinds of work most susceptible to technological unemployment and to layoffs occasioned by temporary cutbacks in production. Furthermore, a larger percentage of the blacks than of the whites in the labor force are recent entrants, who are more

---

88. *Id.* at 3-5.
89. *Id.* at 12.
90. Census Bureau, *supra* note 3, at 56, 69.
91. U.S. Bureau of the Census, *The Social and Economic Status of the Black Population in the United States*, 1973, at 40, Series P-23, No. 48 (1974).
92. Census Bureau, *supra* note 3, at 56, 70.

prone to unemployment than older and more experienced workers. The failure of the incomes of small-scale farm operators to
rise proportionally with the incomes of most other workers has
pushed hundreds of thousands of farmers off the land in recent
years, and a larger percentage of black farmers than of white have
been displaced. The number of jobs in the urban labor force that
these people are qualified to do has not increased rapidly enough
to absorb all the displaced farmers, and thus many are unemployed.[93]

Blacks continued to be overrepresented in lower paying, less skilled
jobs and underrepresented in almost every white collar occupation.
Though only 9 percent of the total employed population, blacks com-
prised 19 percent of all service workers and 17 percent of all nonfarm
laborers in 1974. Within the General System, Wage System, and Postal
Service, the three major pay systems of the federal government, blacks
were concentrated to a greater extent in the lower grades than federal
employees as a whole. There were similar imbalances in black representation in private industry. Whereas blacks made up only about 6
percent of the workers in wholesale and retail trade, and finance,
insurance, and real estate, they were overrepresented in personal service
industries, including private households (21 percent), in health services,
including hospitals (14 percent), in motor vehicles and equipment
manufacturing (13 percent), and in public administration (12 percent).[94]

In 1973, median earnings of black men were substantially below
those of white men in most occupational categories. The Bureau of the
Census quoted median annual earnings of black men working year-
round, full-time in 1973 as $7,880, about 68 percent of the $11,516
earned by white men. However, the earning levels of black women
working at year-round, full-time jobs were relatively closer to those of
white women. The average for black women in 1973 was $5,487, 85
percent of the $6,434 averaged by white women. Earning levels were
nearly equivalent for black and white women in all occupational groups
listed by the Bureau of the Census.[95]

Between 1964 and 1974, however, a greater degree of occupational upgrading did occur among blacks and other minorities than among
whites. The percentage of men of black and other minorities employed
in white-collar jobs, including professional and technical workers, managers and administrators, sales workers, and clerical workers rose from
16 to 24 percent. The largest increase occurred between 1964 and
1970. The percentage of white men in white-collar positions held

---

93. Glenn, *Change in the Social and Economic Conditions of Black Americans
During the 1960's*, in BLACKS IN THE UNITED STATES 48 (N. Glenn & C. Bonjean eds.
1969).
94. Census Bureau, *supra* note 3, at 57, 73-77.
95. *Id.* at 58, 80.

steady at slightly over 40 percent between 1964 and 1974. The proportion of black and other race women in white-collar positions rose more steeply, from 22 percent in 1964 to 42 percent in 1974. Sixteen percent of men of black and other minorities were employed as craft workers in 1974, a rise over 10 years from 12 percent. For white males, the proportion in crafts remained around 20 percent.[96]

The educational differential between blacks and whites continued to narrow, following the pattern of the 1960's.[97] In March, 1973, blacks and other minorities in civilian labor force completed a median of 12.1 school years as compared with a median of 12.5 school years completed by whites. This was a steep increase from the median of 7.6 school years completed by blacks and other minorities in October, 1952. The increase for whites from a 1952 median of 11.4 was slight.[98] Between 1970 and 1974, college enrollment for blacks grew by 56 percent as compared with a 15 percent growth in enrollment for whites.[99] The proportion of high school graduates also rose faster for blacks than for whites within the same period. However, only 72 percent of blacks as compared to 85 percent of whites completed high school. Differentials at the college level were more extreme. Twenty-one percent of white adults completed 4 years of college or more, about two and one-half times the 8.1 percent proportion of blacks at the same level.[100] In 1974, 18 percent of all blacks 18-24 years old were enrolled in college, compared with 25 percent of whites in the same age range; in 1970, the rates were 15 percent and 27 percent, respectively.[101] College enrollment rates for black males continued their rise to 20 percent, while rates for black women leveled off at a slightly lower 16 percent. In 1974, nearly universal school attendance rates existed within the compulsory 6-15 age range.[102]

According to a supplement of the Census Bureau's October, 1973, Current Population Survey, black students were more likely than white students to be enrolled in vocational educational institutions and less likely to be in universities. Whereas the majority of black students were enrolled in public 4-year colleges, white students were enrolled equally in public and private 4-year colleges.[103]

Parity in educational attainment alone, however, will not unravel the knot of racial inequity. A study conducted by Stanley Lieberson and Glenn V. Fuguitt, using a Markov chain to predict consequences, concluded that if black formal education were to reach the same level as

96. Id. at 57, 73-75.
97. Id. at 96.
98. LABOR STATISTICS, supra note 8, at 55-56.
99. Census Bureau, supra note 3, at 92-93.
100. Id. at 96-97.
101. Id. at 94.
102. Id. at 92-94.
103. Id. at 98-99.

that of whites, the effect on black-white occupational equality would still be limited if other sociological factors remained unchanged.[104] Comparisons of the income of blacks and whites with equal levels of educational attainment bear this out. Labor Department statistics for the period 1963-72 indicate that blacks were paid less than whites at all educational levels. In 1972, for example, median income for a black with 4 or more years of college was $14,158, as compared with $18,479 for a white counterpart. In 1972, of those who had completed 4 years of college or more, 32.9 percent of blacks and other minorities earned between $15,000 and $24,999, as compared with 38.7 percent of whites. Among those with 4 or more years of college, whites constituted nearly twice as high a percentage (21.6 percent) of those earning between $25,000 and $49,999 as did blacks and other minorities (11.5 percent).[105]

IV. THE EXISTING LAW AGAINST EMPLOYMENT DISCRIMINATION

It is easy to see from the above data that discrimination against black persons in the job market in this country has been constant and pervasive for nearly 200 years. The pattern of discrimination against blacks has been so persistent that it has become an indelible part of our American heritage.

The price of racial discrimination has been extremely high, in terms of human degradation, racial strife and economic suffering. As W. Mendelson aptly observed in 1962 in his book *Discrimination*:

No man can achieve his full potential as a human being when he is constantly harassed by economic insecurity because of his race—a matter over which he has not the slightest control.

. . . .

Whether direct or indirect, the price of discrimination comes high. Beyond the median cost in human misery and frustration, the public pays exorbitantly. From menial work, job insecurity, and unemployment, the stifling circle of discrimination leads on to slums, family instability, and school drop-outs. This means cultural deprivation, or at best limited opportunity for the informal training of a wholesome environment. At worst it means miseducation, juvenile delinquency, vice, and police brutality. Beyond all this is a waste of human resources, loss of latent skills, and above all a blight on our moral stature.[106]

Despite the costs paid, mostly by minority persons, white persons have all too often been intolerant of black demands for equality, especially in

---

104. Lieberson & Fuguitt, *Negro-White Occupational Differences in the Absence of Discrimination*, in RACIAL DISCRIMINATION IN THE UNITED STATES 203 (T. Pettigrew ed. 1975) [hereinafter cited as Lieberson & Fuguitt].
105. LABOR STATISTICS, *supra* note 8, at 425-35.
106. W. MENDELSON, DISCRIMINATION 70 (1962).

time of serious economic recession. The recent public controversies surrounding welfare programs for the underprivileged, busing to achieve integration in our public schools, and preferential remedies to achieve equal employment opportunity are current examples of "white backlash." But white backlash is not a new phenomenon. White backlash in response to these types of issues has always been with us, and unfortunately, it has usually served to obscure the persistent fact of race discrimination in our society.

One obvious line of attack against the disease of race discrimination is a strong national policy to compel equal employment opportunity for all persons. In the simplest terms, good jobs for minority persons will mean more money, which in turn can buy better housing, decent clothing, and, as we have seen recently, even a good education. A good job helps a person to avoid welfare; it gives a person a sense of worth, well-being and security; and it also utilizes human skills which will help to advance our national economy. In short, real job opportunities can have a meaningful impact in curing some of the worst effects of race discrimination.

When Congress passed Title VII of the Civil Rights Act of 1964,[107] it plainly recognized that employment discrimination against blacks was a critical problem in the United States. It is clear that the entire Civil Rights Act was written with an eye toward the elimination of the "glaring . . . discrimination against Negroes which exists throughout our nation."[108] To emphasize this point, the House Judiciary Report stated that Title VII "can and will commit our Nation to the elimination of many of the worst manifestations of racial prejudice."[109] This notwithstanding, it is also important to recall that Title VII was the *first* significant piece of legislation to prohibit racial discrimination in this country and it did not come until nearly 100 years after the Emancipation Proclamation. What is even more distressing is to recall that even though the Civil Rights Act of 1964 came only after long and "bitter debate" in Congress,[110] Title VII still had to be amended in 1972 to deal with the seemingly irremovable patterns of bias against blacks in the job market. Prior to the enactment of the 1972 amendments to Title VII, the report of the Senate Committee of Labor and Public Welfare noted that:

> Seven years ago, in response to compelling national need and concern, Congress enacted Title VII.

> During the six years since its inception, the EEOC has made an heroic attempt to reduce the incidence of employment discrimination in the Nation, and to ameliorate the conditions which have

---

107.   42 U.S.C. §§ 2000e-1 to 2000e-17 (1970).
108.   H.R. Rep. No. 914, 88th Cong., 1st Sess. 18 (1963).
109.   H.R. Rep. No. 914, 88th Cong., 1st Sess., pt. 2, at 2 (1963).
110.   Bureau of National Affairs, The Civil Rights Act of 1964, at 1 (1964).

led to the persistence of these practices. During this period, however, it has been demonstrated that employment discrimination is even more pervasive and tenacious than the Congress had assumed it to be at the time it passed the Act. . . .[111]

The current panoply of acts and executive orders prohibiting job discrimination in employment is quite varied. Title VII of the Civil Rights Act of 1964, as amended in 1972, makes it an unlawful employment practice to discriminate against any individual on account of the individual's race, color, religion, sex, or national origin. When a violation of the Act is found, a federal district court may, *inter alia*, "order such affirmative action . . . or any other equitable relief as the court deems appropriate."[112]

Employment discrimination is also proscribed by the Civil Rights Acts of 1866 and 1871.[113] The Civil Rights Act of 1866, now 42 U.S.C. Section 1981, has recently been interpreted by the courts to provide a remedy for private acts of employment discrimination.[114] It is narrower than Title VII in that it only applies to race discrimination cases, but it is also broader in that it applies to certain employers who cannot be reached under Title VII. In addition, some of the procedural requirements of Title VII, particularly the time-consuming and cumbersome investigation and conciliation procedures, may be avoidable under section 1981.[115]

The Civil Rights Act of 1871, now 42 U.S.C. Section 1983, proscribes any deprivation of constitutional rights under color of state authority, and it has been interpreted by the courts to provide a remedy for employment discrimination on account of race, sex, or national origin in the public sector.[116] Since, unlike section 1981, section 1983 requires that state action be shown, it does not cover most discrimination in the private sector. As under section 1981, some of the procedural requirements of Title VII can be avoided in a section 1983 suit, and the state statute of limitations is applied.[117]

The necessity for affirmative action to end discrimination has also been recognized under Executive Order 11246, which prohibits employment discrimination on the basis of race, color, religion, sex, and

---

111. Report of Senate Committee on Labor and Public Welfare, *Equal Employment Opportunities Enforcement Act of 1971*, in THE EQUAL EMPLOYMENT OPPORTUNITY ACT OF 1972, at 225, 228 (1973).
112. 42 U.S.C. § 2000e-5(g) (Supp. II 1972), *amending* 42 U.S.C. § 2000e-5(g) (1970).
113. 42 U.S.C. §§ 1981, 1983 (1970).
114. *See, e.g.*, Caldwell v. National Brewing Co., 443 F.2d 1044, 1046 (5th Cir. 1971); Young v. International Tel. & Tel. Co., 438 F.2d 757, 759-60 (3d Cir. 1971).
115. *See generally* Larson, *The Development of Section 1981 as a Remedy for Racial Discrimination in Private Employment*, 7 HARV. CIV. RIGHTS—CIV. LIB. L. REV. 56 (1972).
116. *See, e.g.*, Pennsylvania v. O'Neill, 473 F.2d 1029 (3d Cir. 1973).
117. *See, e.g.*, Madison v. Wood, 410 F.2d 564 (6th Cir. 1969).

national origin by all contractors and all sub-contractors in federal and federally assisted construction.[118]   In addition, there are also a number of state laws in force prohibiting employment discrimination on the basis of race, color, sex, national origin, and age.

Although the current list of laws and orders against employment discrimination is indeed impressive, it would probably be fair to say that the courts (with the help of some very able private attorneys), have been primarily responsible for most of the gains achieved in equal employment opportunity during the past decade.   For one thing, the courts were responsible for reviving the long dormant Civil Rights Acts of 1866 and 1871 and making them effective weapons against employment discrimination in the private and public sectors.   For another thing, the courts have been virtually unwavering in rigidly enforcing the principle of equal employment opportunity.   Following the enactment of Title VII, some of the early court decisions dealing with race discrimination developed a new approach focusing on discriminatory *effects*, rather than intentions, to challenge a great variety of employment practices which excluded minorities from positions in the employment market.   This new interpretive approach reached maturity in the Supreme Court's landmark opinion in *Griggs v. Duke Power Co.*,[119] where the Court stated that:

> The objective . . . of Title VII is . . . to . . . remove barriers that have operated in the past to favor an identifiable group of white employees.   Under the Act, practices, procedures, or tests neutral on their face, and even neutral in terms of intent, cannot be maintained if they operate to "freeze" the status quo of prior discriminatory employment practices. . . .   Congress directed the thrust of the Act to the consequences of employment practices, not simply the motivation. . . .[120]

As a consequence of these developments, the proscription against employment discrimination under Title VII has been an expanding concept, embracing more and more employment practices formerly believed to be sacrosanct.[121]

V.   REMEDIES FOR EMPLOYMENT DISCRIMINATION—
THE NEED FOR PREFERENTIAL TREATMENT

In dealing with employment discrimination cases, the courts and various governmental agencies have demonstrated an awareness that the goal of equal opportunity cannot be effectively implemented solely pursuant to neutral employment practices.   It would seem obvious that

---

118.   3 C.F.R. § 339 (1965), *as amended* by Exec. Order No. 11375, 3 C.F.R. § 684 (1967).

119.   401 U.S. 424 (1971).

120.   *Id.* at 429-30.

121.   *See generally* Edwards, *Substantive Legal Developments Under Title VII*, 79 LAW QUADRANGLE NOTES 11 (1975).

even if all job hiring was hereafter achieved on a nondiscriminatory basis, it would still be years before blacks and women reached a status in the job market comparable to that of white males.[122] Thus, if the pattern of discrimination is to be broken, the present effects of past discrimination must be eliminated. When a company, a government agency, or a union has discriminated against a segment of society for many years, a simple resolution to adopt neutral employment policies will not effectively resolve the problem of race discrimination. Some means of bringing the discriminated-against group up to the level it would have been at but for the discrimination must be employed.

A number of different remedies have been utilized by the courts and various governmental agencies to end employment discrimination. Injunctions have been issued against further discrimination and against strikes or other interferences with plans to end discrimination.[123] The courts have also ordered employers to: disseminate job information specifically aimed at the group discriminated against; keep detailed records to insure nondiscriminatory hiring; hire and provide back pay for individuals who have been victims of discrimination; provide pretest tutoring for job applicants; expand apprenticeship and training programs; and pay punitive damages.[124]

In a number of cases, however, it has been found that these remedies are inadequate to eliminate the effects of proscribed employment bias. Consequently, governmental agencies have used techniques such as affirmative action plans, consent decrees and conciliation agreements, and a number of courts have held that some form of preferential remedy is the most effective means of enforcing equal employment opportunity when the facts show a long history of discrimination against a protected class.[125]

Remedial preferences have been used in a number of different forms.[126] For example, courts have required employers to hire according to ratios of minority to white employees. The employer may be ordered to use the ratio until a certain percentage of the total work force includes minority workers, or the court may compel the employer to adhere to the ratio until a certain number of minority workers are hired. Another form of preferential remedy is "fictional seniority," which provides less senior minority workers protection against layoff or gives

---

122. Lieberson & Fuguitt, *supra* note 104, at 203.
123. *See, e.g.*, NAACP v. Allen, 493 F.2d 614 (5th Cir. 1974); United States v. Carpenters Local 169, 457 F.2d 210 (7th Cir. 1972).
124. *See, e.g.*, Morrow v. Crisler, 491 F.2d 1053 (5th Cir. 1974); United States v. Ironworkers Local 86, 443 F.2d 544 (9th Cir. 1971); Carter v. Gallagher, 452 F.2d 315 (8th Cir. 1971), *modified on rehearing*, 452 F.2d 327.
125. *See, e.g.*, NAACP v. Allen, 493 F.2d 614 (5th Cir. 1974).
126. Meadows v. Ford Motor Co., 510 F.2d 939 (6th Cir. 1975); NAACP v. Allen, 493 F.2d 614 (5th Cir. 1974); Bridgeport Guardians, Inc. v. Bridgeport Civil Service Comm'n, 482 F.2d 1333 (2d Cir. 1973); Delay v. Carling Brewing Co., 10 BNA F.E.P. Cases 164 (N.D. Ga. 1974).

them preferences in promotions or transfers by awarding them more seniority than they would have ordinarily accumulated under existing employment practices. In each instance, the preferential remedy is by definition temporary and it is used only until the habit of discrimination is broken.

As might be expected, many white males have raised vehement protests against preferential remedies in favor of minority or women job applicants. Efforts by the courts and various federal agencies to implement a policy of equal employment opportunity through the use of affirmative action programs, including preferential remedies, received at least grudging support for a number of years, until many people realized that equal rights for minority persons and women would mean increased competition for limited job opportunities. This realization has led to cries of "reverse discrimination" in response to affirmative action and calls for "color blindness" that in reality may be disguised attempts to keep minorities and women from gaining in the job market. The current recession has caused increased interest in the legal, economic, and moral issues surrounding the legitimacy of affirmative action since jobs have become more limited and the hiring of a minority or female may truly be for a position formerly reserved for a white male.

Without regard to whatever else may be said about the underlying moral issues, the evidence heretofore cited with respect to the economic status of blacks in American society makes it obvious that the goal of racial equality will never be reached solely through the neutral principle of color blindness. While the principle of color blindness is "just" in an abstract sense, it has simply failed to effectively alter long-standing patterns of race discrimination in this country. This failure is due, at least in part, to the difficulty involved in proving noncompliance with an order to act in a "neutral" or "non-discriminatory" fashion. More important, ordering an offender to discontinue a discriminatory practice has simply proved ineffectual without supporting affirmative relief. The problem of employment discrimination is still very serious 10 years after the passage of Title VII. In one sense this should not be surprising because practices that have been in existence for 200 years do not disappear easily. Discrimination has become ingrained as a way of life in this country and although much of the conscious discrimination has ceased, the habitual, unconscious patterns of discrimination remain with us today. White males still receive preferences in a number of positions, and minority persons and women still believe that there are many jobs for which they will not be given serious consideration.

Numerous other factors have also contributed to the exclusions of blacks from meaningful positions in the job market. A lack of adequate training is certainly one such factor. It is certainly true that for years blacks have been systematically denied the opportunity to train for the better positions in the employment market. For example, until recently, blacks have not been accepted in the prestigious university graduate programs that serve as the training grounds for many important professional jobs. But the problem is not solely centered around the lack of training opportunities. The continued existence of long-standing myths about the inherent inability of blacks to perform certain work has also contributed to their exclusion from significant jobs in the employment market; discriminatory employment tests have been used to perpetuate the fable of white male superiority; and employer recruitment practices have been effectively used to screen out qualified blacks from both the public and private sectors.[127]

These types of discriminatory practices will never be defeated by neutral policies; this is why progress under the "color blindness" concept has been slow and halting, defeating the promise of equal opportunity made in the original Civil Rights Act of 1964. Given the evidence at hand, it is clear that some forms of preferential remedies, which consider race as a factor in employment decisions, are necessary to break the habit of employment discrimination in the United States.

This is not to say that blacks or women must be thrust into positions for which they are not qualified; however, when the choice is between white males and other qualified or qualifiable individuals, we should open the available positions to those who formerly could not occupy them. Because of the overt preference historically shown for white males in the job market this group has been conditioned to expect and receive a preference over qualified blacks and women. This cycle can only be broken by reversing the preference temporarily until people learn to work with completely neutral criteria.

Several arguments can be put forth to support the claim that the use of preferential remedies is both illogical and unjust. First, it can be argued that, regardless of the traditional preference shown white males in the job market, to now prefer blacks would unfairly punish innocent white males for the misdeeds of their predecessors. Second, it has been contended that white male employees should not suffer in today's job market merely because certain employers were guilty of race discrimination in the past. Finally, it has been claimed that because the blacks and women who may now benefit from job preferences are not the same individuals who were victims of discrimination in the past, they are being rewarded for the wrongs to their ancestors.

These arguments, however, fail to place the preferential remedy in its proper perspective. For one thing, it should be noted that the court ordered preferential remedies are not nearly as widespread as the current debates might suggest. There are relatively few situations in which preferences have been mandated and effectively enforced and in these

---

127. *See generally* Goldschmid, *Black Americans and White Racism: Theory and Research*, in RACIAL DISCRIMINATION IN THE UNITED STATES (T. Pettigrew ed. 1975); THE AMERICAN NEGRO REFERENCE BOOK (J. DAVIS ed. 1966).

few situations the preferential remedies have been carefully circum-scribed.[128] Furthermore, while some may view the preferential remedy as being unfair, some price must be paid to overcome the long-standing and pervasive patterns of race prejudice in this nation. The minor injustice that may be caused by the use of tightly limited preferential remedies is, on balance, outweighed by the fact that temporary preferential remedies appear to be the only way to effectively break the cycle of employment discrimination and open all levels of the job market to all qualified applicants.

The arguments against the use of preferential remedies also over-look an obvious, but crucial factor—preferential remedies are designed to foster, not inhibit, equal employment opportunities. This character-istic distinguishes preferential remedies from the traditional overt dis-crimination in favor of white males—preferential remedies only tempor-arily favor the one group in order to place all individuals on a par. This characteristic also obviates the apparent inconsistency in the argument that in order to end one preference (in favor of white males) other preferences (in favor of minorities and women) must be introduced. Preferential remedies given pursuant to affirmative action to end em-ployment discrimination may be likened to starting one controlled forest fire in order to bring a raging one under control. At first the idea may seem illogical. But the remedial principle is sound; and, of course, if the goal of equal employment opportunity is to be achieved, then we must find remedies that work.

The use of preferential remedies is neither an effort to lower the standards of excellence in any job situation, nor an effort to promote a concept of "reverse discrimination." Preferential remedies merely serve to increase the number of minorities and women in jobs where they have been formally excluded. Affirmative action in general, and preferential remedies in particular, can and do coexist with the maintenance of professional standards in job hiring and retention.

VI. JUDICIALLY IMPOSED LIMITATIONS ON THE USE OF
PREFERENTIAL REMEDIES FOR EMPLOYMENT DISCRIMINATION

Section 703(j) of Title VII[129] forbids the use of preferential treat-ment to remedy an imbalance between minority and nonminority em-ployees. However, a number of courts have found that preferential treatment may be an acceptable remedy for violation of Title VII when there is a history of discrimination, whether the discrimination was intentional or de facto.[130] While some of these opinions fail to mention

---

128. *See* Edwards & Zaretsky, *Preferential Remedies for Employment Discrimination*, 74 MICH. L. REV. 1 (1975).
129. 42 U.S.C. § 2000e-2(j) (1970).
130. *See, e.g.*, Rios v. Steamfitters Local 638, 501 F.2d 622 (2d Cir. 1974); Boston Chapter, NAACP, Inc. v. Beecher, 504 F.2d 1017, 1028 (1st Cir. 1974); Heat & Frost Insulators Local 53 v. Vogler, 407 F.2d 1047 (5th Cir. 1969).

section 703(j),[131] others reason that the section was not intended to prohibit the use of a preferential remedy where an imbalance is a result of past unlawful discrimination.[132]

There is also an implied legislative mandate for the use of preferential remedies under Title VII. Section 703(j) was added to the Civil Rights Act of 1964 as a compromise measure to emphasize that the Act would not require employers to achieve or maintain specific racial balances through the use of preferential treatment. However, at no point in the consideration of the Act did the sponsors indicate that temporary preferential remedies could not be used to overcome the effects of past discrimination.[133] In considering the 1972 amendments to the Civil Rights Act of 1964, Congress impliedly recognized the importance of preferential remedies by rejecting a number of proposed amendments that would have eliminated the use of such remedies. Senator Javits, one of the sponsors of the bill, in arguing against an amendment that would have enjoined all federal officials from requiring preferential remedies, pointed out that the amendment would not only eliminate an important judicial remedy for employment discrimination, but would also preclude effective consent decrees and affirmative action under Executive Order 11246.[134] The Senate rejected the proposed amendment, thereby implying its approval of preferential remedies as employed by the court.

Despite this implied legislative approval of preferential remedies, the courts have continued to subject such remedies to very strict judicial scrutiny. This can be attributed to two factors. First, although section 703(j) has not been interpreted to ban all preferential remedies, it may indicate that the Congress was concerned about the possibility of abuse of such remedies, and therefore that they should not be ordered lightly. Second, Congress has neither affirmatively approved such remedies nor defined the situations in which it might consider their use proper. Preferential treatment is a volatile remedy, and without any specific guidance from the legislature, it is reasonable that the courts would carefully limit the use of these remedies under Title VII and other acts prohibiting employment discrimination.

A careful review of the relevant case law reveals that the courts have imposed substantial limitations on preferential orders to curb employment discrimination. The purpose of ordering preferential treat-

---

131. *See, e.g.,* EEOC v. Detroit Edison Co., 515 F.2d 301 (6th Cir. 1975); United States v. NL Industries, Inc., 479 F.2d 354 (8th Cir. 1973).
132. Rios v. Steamfitters Local 638, 501 F.2d 622, 631 (2d Cir. 1974).
133. The sponsor did indicate that Title VII would not require the maintenance of a racial balance, *see, e.g.,* 110 CONG. REC. 12723 (1964) (Humphrey Explanation); 110 CONG. REC. 7202 (1964) (Justice Dep't Reply), but that is quite different from a temporary preferential remedy used solely to overcome the effects of past discrimination.
134. *See* 118 CONG. REC. 1664 (1972). *See also* 118 CONG. REC. 1661-76 (1972); 118 CONG. REC. 4917-18 (1972).

ment in the employment context is to overcome the effects of past discrimination, not to mandate specific proportions of each race that must be employed. Once the effects of past discrimination are eliminated, the employer may be enjoined from renewing discriminatory practices, but affirmative orders should cease and the employer should no longer be bound by quotas or percentage goals. Virtually every court that has ordered preferential treatment has recognized this and the orders have been formulated to either run for a specific, limited period of time or until a specific, limited percentage or numerical goal is achieved.[135] The goals must be set so that the employer can meet them without hiring unqualified or unqualifiable persons, as a preferential remedy should never force an employer to hire someone who is not otherwise qualified *but for* his or her race or sex. Rather, it should force the employer to hire people who have not been hired *because of* their race or sex.

In determining the upper limit or goal the courts have considered a number of factors. First, some courts have considered the availability of qualified minority persons in the geographic area constituting the job market.[136] The appropriate geographic area is usually defined as the area from which the employer or union has traditionally drawn its employees or members. However, if the traditional job market suggested by the employer or union is unreasonably narrow, so as to exclude a potential pool of minority workers, the court may look at a wider region in determining the employment goal. The goal is typically based on the percentage of minority people in the appropriate job market who could have been employed by the company but for the prior discrimination.

Second, the courts consider the effect that a preferential remedy will have on the company or industry involved and on white male workers. To the extent that any dislocation can be minimized, the courts try to do so.[137]

Third, the availability of training programs for job applicants is considered in determining the preferential goal.[138] The courts do not always require that potential applicants be qualified to do the work immediately, and it is often held sufficient that the pool of applicants be capable of learning the job in a reasonable period of time if that is what was generally required by the company. In such cases, the courts have ordered preferences for training programs as well as for hiring.

---

135. *See, e.g.,* United States v. Lathers Local 46, 471 F.2d 408 (2d Cir. 1973).
136. *E.g.,* Rios v. Steamfitters Local 638, 501 F.2d 622 (2d Cir. 1974); Johnson v. Goodyear Tire & Rubber Co., 491 F.2d 1364 (5th Cir. 1974); Stamps v. Detroit Edison Co., 365 F. Supp. 87, 122 (E.D. Mich. 1973).
137. *E.g.,* Erie Human Relations Comm'n v. Tullio, 493 F.2d 371, 375 (3d Cir. 1974).
138. United States v. Carpenters Local 169, 457 F.2d 210 (7th Cir. 1972); Stamps v. Detroit Edison Co., 365 F. Supp. 87 (E.D. Mich. 1973).

Fourth, preferential remedies only require that the preference be granted to qualified (or qualifiable) persons, and generally assume that all persons within the pool of qualified applicants have equal ability. It would be difficult to rationalize the granting of preferences if a company were able to show that all qualified applicants were not equal, that some were clearly better than others. Therefore, a question can be raised as to whether an employer may avoid the effect of the preferential remedy by "rank ordering" job applicants pursuant to an employment test or some other objective criteria. Several courts have indicated that an employer is entitled to hire the "best qualified" person for a position.[139] Although no case has been found in which rank ordering has been permitted, the best qualified cases make it at least theoretically possible that employers would be able to rank order applicants from best to least qualified.

The problem with rank ordering is that it is difficult, if not impossible, to develop a test that can "rank order" applicants with any degree of certainty, and an invalidated test would presumably fail to satisfy the requirement of a "professionally developed ability test" under Section 703(h) of Title VII.[140] If rank ordering could pass muster under Section 703(h), it would obviously tend to dilute the preferential remedy. But this latter issue has generally been avoided by findings that qualifying examinations were unvalidated and therefore could not legitimately rank applicants; thus, the rank issue is usually a moot question.

Fifth, normally before a preferential remedy is ordered, there is a finding of a history of discrimination against the protected group and a finding that other available relief would be inadequate to overcome the present effect of the discrimination.[141] It is not necessary to show that an employer or union discriminated against minorities; a history of de facto discrimination, the results of which are being perpetuated, is sufficient to establish a prima facie case of discrimination warranting a preferential remedy.[142] The history of discrimination may be inferred from statistics that show a longstanding disparity between the percentage of minority workers available in the job market and the percentage of minority employed.[143] Generally, however, there is also nonstatistical evidence of past and present discrimination. In fact, although statistical evidence alone has been found to be sufficient to support a finding of discrimination under Title VII, research has not disclosed any decisions ordering a preferential remedy upon only a statistical showing

---

139. United States v. Jacksonville Terminal Co., 451 F.2d 418 (5th Cir. 1971); Wilson v. Woodward Iron Co., 362 F. Supp. 886 (N.D. Ala. 1973).
140. 42 U.S.C. § 2000e-2(h) (Supp. IV 1974).
141. *See, e.g.,* Rios v. Steamfitters Local 638, 501 F.2d 622 (2d Cir. 1974); NAACP v. Allen, 493 F.2d 614 (5th Cir. 1974).
142. Erie Human Relations Comm'n v. Tullio, 493 F.2d 371, 373-74 (3d Cir. 1974).
143. Bridgeport Guardians, Inc. v. Bridgeport Civil Serv. Comm'n, 482 F.2d 1333 (2d Cir. 1973).

of discrimination. In addition, if the employer cannot rebut the inference that he has engaged in discrimination, he still may be able to avoid the imposition of a preferential remedy by showing that he has made good faith but unsuccessful efforts to recruit minority persons.

One final factor that seems to enter into decisions on the appropriateness of preferential remedies is the stage at which the employment relation is to be subjected to the remedy. Most of the cases in which preferences have been ordered have involved the hiring of new employees. Although a preference in initial hiring does tend to aid one applicant at the expense of another, neither has a vested right to be hired and there is a less legitimate expectation of favorable action on the part of the white male worker than in other situations, such as promotions based on seniority. In the promotion cases based on seniority, the courts must balance the utility of preferential remedies in ending discrimination against the legitimate expectations of white employees. The court's problem seems to be more acute in promotion and layoff cases, where white males often have long-held expectations, than in the hiring cases where the expectations are less clear.

The courts are split on the advisability of ordering preferences in promotion cases, and the decision in each case may depend on its particular facts. Some courts have noted that an imbalance in higher ranks is often due to discrimination at the entry level of employment, not to promotion per se, so there is no history of discriminatory promotions to correct and correction of hiring discrimination will naturally correct imbalances at higher levels over time.[144] This argument overlooks the importance of ending the effects of discriminatory patterns within a reasonable period of time. Perhaps more persuasive is the argument that when promotion has traditionally had a time-in-grade requirement or has been granted in order of seniority, legitimate career expectations of nonminority workers are thwarted solely because of their race if minority workers are preferred. Many nonminority workers have invested years under the assumption that they would receive promotions under the traditional procedure, and denial of this expectation may have the effect of exacerbating tensions between them and the preferred group. In such cases, it may be wise to reject outright preferences in favor of procedures designed to more indirectly facilitate access to higher level jobs, such as reducing the number of years that must be spent in lower level jobs. Where, on the other hand, there is no legitimate expectation of promotion, for instance where the promotion decision has traditionally been made at the discretion of the company, it is easier to order a preferential remedy. This seems closer to the hiring case, since although there may sometimes be some inequity, nonminority employees are not deprived of a benefit that they had reason to expect.

---

144. *E.g., id.*

VII. THE PROBLEM OF "LAST HIRED, FIRST FIRED"

Analogous to the promotion-by-right problem is the fictional seniority problem that has been raised in layoff cases. Many minority workers, only recently hired under affirmative action programs, have been laid off during the present recession under "last hired, first fired" seniority systems. Thus, it has been claimed that the gains in equal opportunity employment that have been made over the last 10 years are in danger of being lost through layoffs in the recession of the 1970's.

Unfortunately, it is difficult at best to discern the actual impact of last hired, first fired seniority plans on minority employment. Most people have assumed that there is a direct and significant relationship between the current high levels of unemployment among blacks and the existence of last hired, first fired seniority systems. But the data on this point is at best unclear.

In April, 1975, Julius Shiskin, the Commissioner of Labor Statistics at the Department of Labor, reported that most of the rise in unemployment since the recession began in 1973 has been due to layoffs. But Shiskin also suggested that it difficult to tell which population group (that is, black or whites) has had the greater percentage increase in number of laid off workers since the start of the recession.[145] It is true that, in absolute terms, there is no comparison between the number of unemployed black versus white workers. The rate of unemployment for blacks has remained at nearly twice the rate of white workers during the entire recession. However, in determining the percentage increase in the number of workers laid off, the figures vary depending upon the base period that is used. The United States economy was at a peak during the third quarter of 1973 and the current recession began in the fourth quarter of 1973. From the fourth quarter of 1973 through the first quarter of 1975, the number of black male workers laid off increased at a faster rate than that for whites—169.3 percent versus 146.3 percent.[146] However, the opposite result is found if the third quarter of 1973 is used as the base period for measurement. From the third quarter of 1973 through the first quarter of 1975, the percentage increase in laid off workers was 171.6 percent for white males and 139.8 per cent for blacks. Shiskin reported other similar variations in the percentage figures over different time periods and concluded that "Blacks have been hit about as hard as Whites by layoffs."[147]

The figures do indeed suggest that blacks and whites have been affected about the same by layoffs during the current recession. However, this does not mean that black and white persons have suffered

---

145. Washington Post, Apr. 24, 1975, at A1, col. 5; *id.*, Apr. 29, 1975, at A2, col. 1.
146. *Id.*
147. *Id.*

equally during the recession; in fact, nothing could be further from the truth, because blacks were in a substantially worse position in the first place. But the Department of Labor figures are still important because they do question how much of a detrimental impact "last hired, first fired" seniority systems have had on minority employment during the 1973-75 recession.

It is interesting to recall that the same issues were raised with respect to the principle of "last hired, first fired" and black employment during the 1960 recession. Wallace Mendelson, in his book *Discrimination*,[148] observed that:

> Every recession demonstrates the old adage that the Negro is the first fired and the last hired. The Negro unemployment rate in the 1960 decline, for example, was roughly double that for whites. In industrial centers the disparity was greater. Thus in Detroit where Negroes account for only 19% of the work force, they constituted 61% of the unemployed. To put it differently, they suffered an unemployment rate three times greater than that of the city as a whole.
>
> Entirely apart from direct discrimination, it is often merely "seniority" that handicaps Negroes because of their recent arrival upon the industrial scene. More important, they are generally concentrated in the lower and unskilled jobs. And it is precisely there that cyclical and technological layoffs hit hardest. Moreover, many who lose their jobs for recession reasons never get them back because of changing industrial techniques. The result is apt to be chronic or permanent unemployment.[149]

Mendelson's point about blacks being confined to the lowest jobs, where cyclical layoffs hit the hardest, is a crucial consideration. The principle of last hired, first fired surely does affect these positions because they are normally found in large industrial sectors covered by major collective bargaining agreements. But, again, it is not clear to what extent black workers as opposed to white workers are actually adversely affected by last hired, first fired seniority systems under existing union contracts. This is especially true in settings like the steel industry where a good number of long-service blacks are protected by high plant seniority.

It is probably fair to say that the ultimate impact of cyclical recessions on affirmative action programs depends on a number of factors, including the frequency and severity of the recessions, the relative seniority of minority workers, and the number who either are not recalled or forfeit their recall rights.[150] It is possible and indeed probable that some minority workers will survive each recession without a layoff and that a number will be recalled and returned to work when

---

148. W. MENDELSON, DISCRIMINATION (1962).
149. *Id.* at 69.
150. *See generally*, Note, *Last Hired, First Fired Layoffs and Title VII*, 88 HARV. L. REV. 1544 (1975).

the economy swings upward, then accumulating seniority which will make them more resistant to layoff in the next downturn. Thus, the most likely effect of cyclical recession is to slow, but not to completely halt, the achievement of minority employment goals.

The further importance of the point made by Mendelson is that blacks have traditionally been excluded from the relatively "safe" white collar, technical and professional jobs, where the effects of a cyclical recession are usually less severe. It is precisely because there have never been significant numbers of blacks in these "better" jobs that (1) the rate of unemployment for blacks has remained at a substantially higher level than the rate for whites during both periods of prosperity and recession and (2) the overall impact of the current recession has clearly had a greater adverse effect on black persons in our society.

Whatever may be the actual impact of last hired, first fired seniority systems on minority employment during the current recession, the courts are split on the question of whether to grant "fictional seniority" to minority workers in order to insulate them from layoffs.[151] It is clear that many minority workers hired during the last decade pursuant to the legal mandate of equal employment opportunity have been the first persons laid off when employers have applied last hired, first fired during the current recession. Thus, a number of courts have been faced with the issue whether such layoffs, which frequently have a disproportionate impact on black workers in a given employment setting, violate Title VII or other laws prohibiting job bias on the basis of race. The issue arises because in many cases it has been asserted that black workers would have been hired earlier, and thus attained superior seniority ranking, but for the prior discrimination. Thus, in these cases, the application of last hired, first fired has in a very real sense perpetuated the adverse effects of prior discrimination against blacks in the job market.

Those courts that have granted fictional seniority have reasoned that since minority workers would have been hired years earlier but for race discrimination, it is not improper to grant fictional seniority to put them in the position in which they would have been absent historical discrimination. However, since the effect of such a remedy is to cause the displacement of white male employees in favor of minority employees, it directly conflicts with the oft-cited dictum in *United Papermakers & Paperworkers Local 189 v. United States.*[152] In that decision, the

---

151. *Compare* Delay v. Carling Brewing Co., 10 BNA F.E.P. Cases 164 (N.D. Ga. 1974); Schaefer v. Tannian, 10 BNA F.E.P. Cases 897 (E.D. Mich. 1974); Loy v. City of Cleveland, 8 BNA F.E.P. Cases 614, *dismissed as moot*, 8 BNA F.E.P. Cases 617 (N.D. Ohio 1974); *with* Watkins v. United Steelworkers of America Local 2369, 10 BNA F.E.P. Cases 1297 (5th Cir. 1975); Jersey Cent. Power & Light Co., v. IBEW, 9 BNA F.E.P. Cases 117 (3d Cir. 1975); Waters v. Wisconsin Steel Works, 502 F.2d 1309 (7th Cir. 1974).

152. 416 F.2d 980 (5th Cir. 1969).

Fifth Circuit stated in effect that employees with real seniority (that is, with actual time worked with the company) could never be displaced by less senior employees pursuant to a court order altering an existing seniority system:

Creating fictional employment time for newly hired Negroes would comprise preferential rather than remedial treatment. The clear thrust of the Senate debate [concerning Section 703(h) and (j)] is directed against such preferential treatment on the basis of race.[153]

However, the court in *Papermakers* did uphold the district court's order creating a company-wide seniority system in place of the preexisting departmental seniority system. This had been done in order to minimize the residual effects of a formerly segregated department structure, which was being perpetuated by a departmental seniority system under which only time worked in a department was credited towards seniority in the department. The court seemed persuaded that the company-wide seniority system was a reasonable way to preserve "the earned expectation of long-service employees" while reducing their discriminatory effects, and that it would be unfair to more fully deprive nonminority employees of such expectations in order to further the goal of equal opportunity.

Actually, the fictional seniority problem must be divided into two parts. First, there is the problem of the appropriate remedy for individuals who have suffered specific instances of discrimination. For example, a minority person who applied for a job 2 years ago and was rejected because of race would most likely be ordered hired and given back pay for the 2-year period. But if a company using a last hired, first fired seniority system decides to lay off some workers, the same minority employee, recently hired but who should have been hired 2 years earlier, will have no seniority and will be the first to go. In such a case, where the specific discriminatees can be identified, retroactive seniority should be granted. The white male workers who might be disadvantaged are not really being treated unfairly because they will be in exactly the same position as that in which they would have been but for the discrimination. While it may be true that white males should not be prejudiced by the company's past discrimination, there is no reason why they should retain an unearned advantage. Besides, the retroactive seniority remedy, when limited to identifiable discriminatees, would have no effect on most employees, since the basic seniority system would be left intact.

Some support for this position may be found in the Supreme Court's recent decision in *Albemarle Paper Company v. Moody*,[154] where the Court discussed the standards by which back pay should be

---

153.   *Id.* at 995.
154.   95 S. Ct. 2362 (1975).

awarded after proof of a violation of Title VII. First, the Court made it clear that Title VII "requires that persons aggrieved by the consequences and effects of the unlawful practice be, so far as possible, restored to a position where they would have been were it not for the unlawful discrimination."[155] Second, the Court observed that the remedial provisions of Title VII were fashioned after the remedial provisions of the National Labor Relations Act and should therefore be construed in a manner consistent with the case precedent under the NLRA. Reinstatement with back pay and with retroactive seniority rights is a common remedy for victims of unfair labor practices under the NLRA.[156] Although many of the NLRA cases have involved discriminatory discharges, the NLRB has also awarded retroactive seniority to victims of unlawful discrimination in refusal to hire cases.[157] Thus, in following the suggestions made by the Supreme Court in *Albemarle* that victims of unlawful discrimination should be "restored to a position where they would have been were it not for the unlawful discrimination" and that the case law under NLRA should be followed in developing remedies under Title VII, it may be contended that persons who have been unlawfully denied job rights at the hiring stage of employment should be awarded both back pay and retroactive seniority under Title VII.

The issue of retroactive seniority for "identifiable discriminatees" will be resolved this term by the Supreme Court when it decides *Franks v. Bowman Transportation Co.*[158] In *Franks*, the District Court found that the company had discriminated against certain black applicants by denying them jobs as over-the-road truck drivers because of their race. On appeal to the Fifth Circuit, the Court of Appeals considered whether the black persons who were identified as the victims of past hiring discrimination should be awarded seniority retroactive to the date when they had first applied for and been denied jobs due to race bias. In rejecting the request for retroactive seniority, the court relied primarily on the dictum in the *Papermakers* case[159] to the effect that "constructive seniority" was impermissible as a remedy under section 703(h) of Title VII. However, the reference to section 703(h) by the Fifth Circuit seems clearly misplaced in *Franks*. Section 703(h) merely states that

155. *Id.* at 2373, *quoting* 118 CONG. REC. 7168 (1972) (remarks of Sen. Williams).
156. *E.g.*, NLRB v. Lone Star Textiles, Inc., 386 F.2d 535 (5th Cir. 1967); Ventre Packing Co., Inc., 163 NLRB 540, 543 (1967); West Boylston Mfg. Co., 87 NLRB 808, 813 (1949).
157. *E.g.*, Aclang, Inc., 193 NLRB 86 (1971); Bob's Casing Crews, 178 NLRB 3 (1969).
158. 495 F.2d 398 (5th Cir. 1974), *rev'd*, 44 U.S.L.W. 4356 (Mar. 24, 1976) (No. 74-728). The Supreme Court concluded that Congress, in enacting § 703(h), did not intend to modify or restrict relief that is otherwise appropriate once an illegal discriminatory practice is proven. The Court then held that granting retroactive seniority § 706(g) is an appropriate make-whole remedy.
159. *See* United Papermakers & Paperworkers Local 189 v. United States, 416 F.2d 980 (5th Cir. 1969).

"[n]otwithstanding any other provisions of this title it shall not be an unlawful employment practice for an employer to apply different standards of compensation, or different terms, conditions, or privileges of employment pursuant to a bona fide seniority or merit system. . . ." Nothing in section 703(h) precludes the granting of retroactive seniority to an identified victim of discrimination who has been denied an actual job due to race bias. Indeed, it seems clear that the only way that such a person can be "made whole" for the prior act of discrimination is to be given the seniority standing that he or she would have had *but for* the unlawful act of discrimination. This is precisely the rationale followed by the NLRB and labor arbitrators who routinely reinstate employees who are victims of improper discharges under the NLRA or "just cause" provisions in collective bargaining agreements.

The court in *Franks* also cited *Papermakers* for the proposition that "[c]reating fictional employment time for newly hired Negroes would constitute preferential rather than remedial treatment."[160] However, this statement ignores two important considerations: first, as shown above, the courts have frequently recognized that "preferential remedies" may in fact be remedial in many cases; and second, the "retroactive seniority" remedy is not the same "fictional seniority." As one writer has noted:

> Retroactive seniority is "fictional" only in the same sense that most other standard remedies for Title VII violations are fictional. . . . One may reasonably ask whether back pay is any less "fictional" than retroactive seniority. Is pay for time not actually worked any different conceptually from seniority for time not actually worked?[161]

Another recent case involving a claim for retroactive seniority for identifiable victims of discrimination was decided by the Sixth Circuit in *Meadows v. Ford Motor Co.*[162] The Sixth Circuit opinion, unlike the Fifth Circuit decision in *Franks*, plainly recognizes that "there is . . . no provision to be found in [Title VII] . . . which prohibits retroactive seniority." However, the Sixth Circuit opinion is hardly unequivocal on this point. In remanding the case to the District Court for further consideration, the Sixth Circuit made the following significant observations:

> Whatever the difficulties of determining back pay awards, the award of retroactive job seniority offers still greater problems. Seniority is a system of job security calling for reduction of work forces in periods of low production by layoff first of those employees with the most recent dates of hire. It is justified among work-

---

160.   495 F.2d at 417-18, *citing* 416 F.2d 980, 995 (5th Cir. 1969).
161.   Friedman & Katz, *Retroactive Seniority for the Identifiable Victim Under Title VII—Must Last Hired First Fired Give Way?*, PROCEEDINGS OF THE 28TH ANN. CONFERENCE ON LABOR (1975).
162.   510 F.2d 939 (6th Cir. 1975).

ers by the concept that the older workers in point of service have earned their retention of jobs by the length of prior services for the particular employer. From the employer's point of view, it is justified by the fact that it means retention of the most experienced and presumably most skilled of the work force. Obviously, the grant of fully retroactive seniority would collide with both of these principles.

In addition, where the burden of the retroactive pay falls upon the party which violated the law, the burden of retroactive seniority for determination of layoff would fall exactly upon other workers who have themselves had no hand in the wrongdoing found by the District Court.

. . . [A] grant of retroactive seniority would not depend solely upon the existence of a record sufficient to justify back pay. . . . The Court would, in dealing with job seniority, need also to consider the interest of the workers who might be displaced as well as the interest of the employer in retaining an experienced work force.[163]

Although the court in *Meadows* concedes that retroactive seniority may be an appropriate remedy for identifiable victims of employment discrimination under Title VII, some of the language in the opinion is troublesome. For example, the court's concern about white workers being displaced as a consequence of a grant of retroactive seniority to black victims of employment discrimination is somewhat difficult to understand. The likelihood of job displacement among white employees is no greater in the retroactive seniority case than it is in the departmental or job seniority type case seen in *Papermakers*.[164] When a court finds that a departmental or job seniority system is unlawful under Title VII and allows black workers to exercise plant-wide seniority to move into jobs formerly closed to them, the expectations of white employees are surely denied. While it is true that the courts have never condoned *direct* job displacement of white employees in the departmental or job seniority cases, it is important to recognize that an *indirect* form of job displacement has been allowed as a consequence of the remedial orders issued in these cases. A simple hypothetical example will suffice to demonstrate this point:

Under job seniority, a white worker with 6 years seniority on the "job" and 6 years in the plant would have superior rights to the "job" over a black worker with zero years on the job and 15 years in the plant. If, however, a court finds that the job seniority system is unlawful under Title VII, and orders the substitution of plant-wide seniority in place of job seniority, then the respective rights of the white and black workers will be significantly altered. It is true that the black worker will not be allowed to bump or displace the white worker from his job; however, the black employee

---

163. *Id.* at 948-49.
164. *See* note 148 *supra*.

will be allowed to fill any vacancy in the job on the basis of his plant-wide seniority. If the black worker elects to do this and if both the white and black workers are subsequently laid off, the black worker (with greater plant seniority) will have superior rights over the white worker to recall. Thus, if upon recall there is only one job left, the black worker will displace the white worker who formerly had superior job seniority to him.

This example should amply indicate that the courts have indeed at least implicitly condoned job displacement in the departmental and job seniority cases. No less should be done in the cases involving claims for retroactive seniority by persons who have been identified as victims of discrimination at the hiring stage of employment.

The most difficult problems in the so-called retroactive or fictional seniority cases arise when a company with a long history of discrimination finally starts hiring blacks and none of the minority persons hired are specific discriminatees. In such cases, if the employer subsequently finds it necessary to cut back the work force, and fictional seniority is granted to the recently hired minority persons, white employees who had an expectation of continued employment or promotion based on their seniority will be denied their expectations because of their race. However, if the remedy is denied, a round of layoffs can restore the earlier imbalance among minority employees.

Thus far, the three Courts of Appeal that have dealt with this problem, in the Third, Fifth, and Seventh Circuits,[165] have all followed the dictum of the *Papermakers* decision and have refused to alter last hired, first fired layoff systems even though the effect of these systems was to deny rehire to a disproportionate number of recently hired, low seniority minority persons.

The first such opinion was rendered by the Seventh Circuit in *Waters v. Wisconsin Steel Works of International Harvester Co.*[166] The *Waters* case is somewhat complicated by a cumbersome record of facts. The plaintiff, Mr. Waters, initially applied for and was denied employment with the company in 1957. Waters was subsequently hired by the company in July, 1964, but he was laid off due to a reduction in the work force in September, 1964. Later, in March of 1965, thirty white employees, some with considerable seniority, were also laid off due to a further reduction in the work force. Waters filed a complaint with the Equal Employment Opportunity Commission in May, 1966, charging that the company had unlawfully discriminated against him when it laid him off and then refused to rehire him. In June, 1966, the company and the bricklayers union agreed to amend an earlier severance pay agreement and thereby recall three white bricklayers who had previously terminated their employment with the company and had accepted sever-

---

165. *See* note 147 *supra.*
166. 502 F.2d 1309 (7th Cir. 1974).

ance pay under the initial agreement. The Court of Appeals found that Waters would have been recalled to his former bricklayer job in January, 1967, but for the June, 1966, severance agreement which allowed these three white employees to return to work ahead of the plaintiff. Waters was finally recalled to his job in March, 1967, but he was laid off again in May, 1967. He was recalled again a third time in September, 1967, but he declined to return to his old job at that time.

After reviewing all the pertinent facts, the Seventh Circuit found that "the record supports the conclusion that Wisconsin Steel engaged in racially discriminatory hiring policies with respect to the position of bricklayer prior to the enactment of Title VII."[167] It is noteworthy, however, that although the court found that the company was guilty of discrimination against blacks prior to 1964, there was no specific finding that the company had denied Waters an actual job in the bricklayer position prior to 1964. Apparently on the basis of this evidence, the court concluded as follows:

> It would appear from the record that but for the June 1966 agreement, Waters would have been recalled on January 17, 1967, and that he would not have been laid off on May 19, 1967. Waters was tendered reemployment on September 5, 1967, which he declined to accept. In our judgment the discriminatory impact of defendants' June 1966 agreement ended with the tender made to Waters in September. The relevant period for computing damages therefore ranges from January 17, 1967, to September 5, 1967.[168]

However, on the question of retroactive seniority (or "fictional seniority," as the court put it), the court relied strictly on the dictum in the *Papermakers* decision:

> We are of the view that Wisconsin Steel's employment seniority system embodying the "last hired, first fired" principle of seniority is not of itself racially discriminatory or does it have the effect of perpetuating prior racial discrimination in violation of the strictures of Title VII. To that end we find the legislative history of Title VII supportive of the claim that an employment seniority system is a "bona fide" seniority system under the Act. . . .
>
> . . . .
>
> Title VII mandates that workers of every race be treated equally according to their earned seniority. It does not require as the Fifth Circuit said, that a worker be granted fictional seniority or special privileges because of his race.
>
> . . . .
>
> Title VII speaks only to the future. Its backward gaze is found only on a present practice which may perpetuate past discrimination. An employment seniority system embodying the

---

167. *Id.* at 1316.
168. *Id.* at 1321.

"last fired, first fired" principle does not of itself perpetuate past discrimination. To hold otherwise would be tantamount to shackling white employees with a burden of a past discrimination created not by them but by their employer. Title VII was not designed to nurture such reverse discriminatory practices.[169]

The court's suggestion that last hired, first fired does not perpetuate past discrimination is sheer nonsense. It may be that the court was unwilling to extend Title VII to cover the so-called pure fictional seniority cases, but it surely cannot be found that the last hired, first fired seniority system in *Waters* did not perpetuate the effects of past discrimination.

The court's use of the term fictional seniority is also seemingly misplaced in *Waters*. Actually, it would appear that the case involved a claim for retroactive seniority by a person who was allegedly denied a job on an unlawful basis. The real issue in the case, which is not resolved, is whether Waters was actually discriminated against in 1957. Although the court found a pattern of discrimination against blacks in the bricklayer position, it did not find that the plaintiff was specifically denied an actual job position in 1957. Therefore, it is not clear that this case falls into the category of cases like *Franks*[170] and *Meadows*[171] involving identifiable discriminatees. (That is, there is no evidence to show that Waters was actually discriminated against in 1957 on the basis of his race or that he was discouraged from applying for a job because of the company's discriminatory policies.) This being the case, it would appear that the *Waters* decision is very much like the decisions rendered by the Third and Fifth Circuits in *Jersey Central*[172] and *Watkins*.[173]

In *Jersey Central Power & Light Co. v. IBEW*,[174] the Third Circuit reversed a District Court order that would have granted fictional seniority to women and minority employees to protect earlier affirmative action gains during periods of layoffs. The Court of Appeals noted that section 703(h) of Title VII on its face enjoins the courts from interfering with a bona fide seniority system, and "conclude[d] in light of the [section's] legislative history that on balance a facially neutral company-wide seniority system, *without more*, is a bona fide seniority system [which] will be sustained even though it may operate to the disadvantage of females and minority groups as a result of past employment practices."[175]

---

169. *Id.* at 1318-20.
170. Franks v. Bowman Transp. Co., 495 F.2d 398 (5th Cir. 1974), *rev'd*, 44 U.S.L.W. 4356 (Mar. 24, 1976) (No. 74-728).
171. Meadows v. Ford Motor Co., 510 F.2d 939 (6th Cir. 1975).
172. 508 F.2d 687 (3d Cir. 1975).
173. Watkins v. United Steelworkers Local 2369, 516 F.2d 41 (5th Cir. 1975).
174. 508 F.2d 687 (3d Cir. 1975).
175. *Id.* at 710.

Actually, the Third Circuit opinion is quite different from and less significant than the decisions rendered by the Seventh and Fifth Circuits in *Waters* and *Watkins*, respectively. In *Jersey Central*, the employer, when faced with the necessity of laying off a number of employees for economic reasons, sought a declaratory judgment defining its rights and obligations under (1) a collective bargaining agreement between it and several unions and (2) a conciliation agreement involving the EEOC, the employer, and the unions. Given this setting, the Court of Appeals viewed the proceeding primarily as one involving the interpretation of contracts and it declined to consider the issue of past employment practices of either the company or the unions. Rather, the Third Circuit merely ruled that the labor and conciliation agreements did not conflict and that the conciliation agreement, which provided for affirmative action in favor of minority persons and women, actually incorporated the concept of last hired, first fired as embodied in the seniority provision of the collective bargaining contract.

Probably the best known case among this trilogy of Courts of Appeal decisions is the case of *Watkins v. United Steelworkers Local 2369*.[176] In *Watkins*, the District Court found that the legislative history surrounding section 703(h) did not clearly preclude the granting of a preferential remedy (fictional seniority) in a layoff situation.[177] The court observed that the interpretive comments regarding seniority were made during the Senate debates prior to the time when section 703(h) was inserted into Title VII, and therefore concluded that these remarks could not be considered determinative in construing the statute. Rather, the court ruled that section 703(h) literally protected only bona fide seniority systems and that a system perpetuating the effects of past discrimination could not be bona fide. The District Court also rejected the *Papermakers* dictum as mere "remarks . . . made without the benefit of adversary arguments,"[178] and noted that since the Fifth Circuit in *Papermakers* had altered an existing seniority system in order to desegregate various jobs within a company, there was no reason why a company that had refused to hire blacks at all should be allowed to perpetuate effects of that discrimination through its seniority rules. Thus, the court in effect found that any detriment to nonminority employees was, on balance, outweighed by the need to overcome the effects of past discrimination against blacks. This position is consistent with the recently adopted interpretive ruling rendered by the Equal Employment Opportunity Commission.

However, the District Court decision in *Watkins* was subsequently reversed by the Fifth Circuit.[179] The Fifth Circuit held that neither

176. 516 F.2d 41 (5th Cir. 1975).
177. 369 F. Supp. 1221, 1228-29 (E.D. La. 1974).
178. *Id.* at 1229.
179. 516 F.2d 41 (5th Cir. 1975).

Title VII nor section 1981 of the Civil Rights Act of 1866 bars the use of a long-established seniority system, adopted without intent to discriminate, to determine which employees should be laid off, even though minority employee balance is adversely affected. But the court noted as part of its deliberately narrow holding that the employer's hiring practices had been nondiscriminatory for over 10 years and that none of the individual employees laid off had personally been the victim of prior employment discrimination. The court

> [S]pecifically [did] not decide the rights of a laid-off employee who could show that, but for the discriminatory refusal to hire him at an earlier time than the date of his actual employment, or but for his failure to obtain earlier employment because of exclusion of minority employees from the work force, he would have sufficient seniority to insulate him against layoff.[180]

The decision in *Watkins* is important not so much because it follows the dictum of *Papermakers,* but rather because it leaves open the possibility that retroactive seniority, as opposed to fictional seniority, may still be used as a legitimate remedy for past discrimination under Title VII. The court in *Watkins* was careful to stress throughout its opinion that the plaintiffs were not the victims of discrimination prior to 1965. On this point, the court noted that:

> Age, not race, is the principal reason the plaintiffs in this case did not have sufficient seniority to withstand layoff. All but one were under the age of legal employment when the Company commenced equal hiring. No plaintiff has alleged that he applied for employment with the Company prior to 1965 and was rejected for discriminatory reasons or that he would have applied for employment but for the discriminatory hiring practices of the Company. During the working lifetime of these plaintiffs, there has been no history of discrimination, and none of them has suffered individual discrimination at the hand of the Company.[181]

Given these facts, the court was primarily concerned about the problem of "reverse discrimination" against white employees: "To hold the seniority plan discriminatory as to the plaintiffs in this case requires a determination that blacks not otherwise personally discriminated against should be treated preferentially over equal whites."[182] This concern about the problem of reverse discrimination is not without some merit; however, the Fifth Circuit opinion in *Watkins* fails to distinguish the numerous cases in which preferential hiring remedies have been issued by the courts to correct racial discrimination in employment. The main point here is that the white job applicants who lose out in the normal preferential hiring cases have no greater claim to the jobs than the black persons who are hired pursuant to court order, whereas in the *Watkins*

---

180. *Id.* at 45.
181. *Id.* at 46.
182. *Id.*

case the white employees had superior job rights by virtue of the existing neutral seniority system.

The court in *Watkins* hedged on the question of the meaning of legislative history of section 703(h) in Title VII and ruled instead that:

It is quite apparent that, regardless of what that history may show as to Congressional intent concerning the validity of seniority systems as applied to persons who have themselves suffered from discrimination, there was an express intent to preserve contractual rights of seniority as between whites and persons who had not suffered any effects of discrimination.[183]

The legislative history of section 703(h) suggests that whether or not Congress actually meant to prohibit fictional seniority as a remedy under Title VII it did not intend to affirmatively endorse that remedy.[184] In the absence of any clear legislative mandate, the courts probably should at least scrutinize the layoff/fictional seniority cases very carefully and attempt to find some other means of handling the problem. Part of the problem when there are no specific discriminatees is that there is no way to determine whether the workers who benefit from fictional seniority are the same workers who were hurt by the company's (and/or union's) prior discrimination, and conversely, there is no way to tell how much the nonminority workers benefited from the discrimination. In many cases there will be no correlation for either minority or nonminority workers between their individual positions and the discrimination.

Although the same problem exists to some extent in the preferential hiring cases, it is less serious in those cases because they do not thwart the long standing expectations of nonminority workers and are not likely to create as much tension. Thus, although hiring preferences are strictly scrutinized, fictional seniority cases should be even more strictly scrutinized with an eye toward working out some compromise that would thwart neither the white male's job expectations nor the movement towards equal employment opportunity.

VIII. ALTERNATIVE SOLUTIONS TO FICTIONAL SENIORITY

Given the present composition of the Supreme Court, the uniformity of the opinions among the three courts of appeal that have thus far dealt with the issue, and the numerous difficult legal and moral questions raised by the problem of fictional seniority, it is unlikely that the Supreme Court will overturn the precedents established by *Waters*, *Jersey Central* and *Watkins*. Possibly in recognition of this fact, and surely in an effort to offer useful remedies for a severe national problem, a number of scholars, practitioners and politicians have recently pro-

---

183. *Id.* at 48.
184. *See* 110 CONG. REC. 7217 (1964). *See also* 110 CONG. REC. 7207 (1964); 110 CONG. REC. 7212-15 (1064); 110 CONG. REC. 6563-64 (1964).

posed alternative solutions to the problem of last hired, first fired. Although there may be reason to be cynical about these alternative solutions—since many have been suggested in times past and none appear to be fool proof—still it would be irresponsible to simply ignore them. The fictional seniority remedy appears doomed and, therefore, alternative remedies must be considered. If nothing else, a consideration of some of the alternative remedies may reveal the true level of the commitment to the principle of equal employment opportunity in American society.

A.   The UAW Position: Guaranteed Recall and "Front Pay"

Not surprisingly, most union officials object strenuously to any erosion of the seniority principle. As a consequence, very few union leaders favor the concept of fictional seniority, expecially if it can be used against workers with greater actual seniority in a period of economic recession.

The UAW, although long an advocate of equal employment opportunity, is a good example of a traditional union that is strongly opposed to fictional seniority. The official UAW position has been stated as follows:

> Let us see what would happen if [a] hundred worker plant (sixty whites and forty minorities) were a U.A.W. plant, under a U.A.W. contract. Under the seniority and recall rights retention provision of the agreement, the forty minority workers would be laid off, because they were last hired and had the least seniority— *but they would be laid off, not fired. "Last hired, first fired" applies only to non-union plants.* The minority workers would still be employees of the company with a contractual relationship between them and the employer. They would have a series of enforceable rights. Most importantly, each would have the right to be recalled when production increases. Each would have the right to valuable economic benefits while still on layoff, such as SUB, insurance, and vested vacation pay, depending on the agreement and their length of seniority. . . .
>
> And consider the two situations in terms of affirmative action. In the union situation, though laid off, the minority employees are still employees of that employer with enforceable, valuable, contractual rights, including the right to return to work. It is no empty thing, therefore, to say that they are still in the work force and the sixty-forty ratio achieved through affirmative action has been preserved. In the non-union situation the minority workers are gone forever and the affirmative action ratio has shrunk to zero.
>
> Most union contract seniority provisions include the so-called time-for-time principle, under which recall rights are lost if the layoff lasts longer than the worker's seniority. Even in the union situation . . . a long layoff might have the effect of severing the

minority worker's employment relationship. Therefore, it is the U.A.W.'s position that affirmative action orders or agreements which apply to a union contract situation should include a provision guaranteeing that no employee's employment relationship can be terminated as a result of a long layoff.[185]

When carefully evaluated, it is plain to see that the UAW proposal is at best a modest concession to minority workers who must suffer through a recession without employment. For one thing, the proposal fails to deal with the enormous category of non-union workers. For another thing, while it is true that the right to "recall" is not an insignificant point, it is hardly a major consideration for a person who is suffering without a job during a period of economic recession. It must be recognized that not all union contracts provide for supplemental unemployment benefits; even when available, SUB benefits are but a percentage of a worker's normal take-home pay; neither SUB benefits nor unemployment benefits are guaranteed for unlimited periods; vacation and other like fringe benefits normally are not paid to unemployed workers; unemployed workers lose the opportunity to train for higher skilled jobs; and unemployed workers always risk the possibility of permanent job displacement in the event that the employer closes down a part of the operation. Thus, the right of recall referred to in the UAW position is at best a small gain for the unemployed minority worker.

With respect to the problem of the "identifiable discriminatee," the UAW has proposed a somewhat novel remedy, entitled "front pay." The UAW front pay remedy is constructed as follows:

> [A minority worker who has been discriminated against at the hiring stage of employment] should receive, in addition to a job and back pay from the employer, all back seniority rights except those used against other employees in layoff and recall. In addition, any such discriminatee who is caught in a layoff in which he or she would not have been caught but for the employer's hiring gate discrimination, should continue to be paid full wages and fringes for the period of the layoff, or that part of it he or she could have avoided but for the employer's original refusal to hire him or her.[186]

Again, it may be seen that the UAW position rigidly rejects any form of fictional or retroactive seniority that might be used against workers with actual seniority in a period of economic recession. The front pay remedy plainly does afford the minority worker some significant economic protection against layoff, but it effectively limits the right of the employer to reduce the work force during low production. It is because of this latter impact that the front pay remedy will probably be rejected by the courts. A modified version of the front pay remedy was

185. 27 UAW ADMINISTRATIVE LETTER (No. 3, Aug. 12, 1975).
186. *Id.*

adopted by the District Court in the *Watkins* case, but rejected on appeal by the Fifth Circuit.

B.   Inverse Seniority

Another proposal that has been suggested as an alternative to fictional seniority is "inverse seniority." This suggestion, which was recently advanced by Robert Lund, Dennis Bumstead, and Sheldon Friedman in the September-October, 1975, edition of the *Harvard Business Review*,[187] contemplates inverting the order in which people are laid off as a method of solving the last hired, first fired problem. To implement this proposal, Lund and Bumstead suggest that:

> The most senior eligible person [be] permitted to elect temporary layoff in the place of the junior worker who normally would be subject to layoff. While on layoff, the senior person receives compensation—normally more than the amount provided by state unemployment compensation—and has the right to return to his previous job. Through this approach, it is possible to retain more people in junior ranks where disadvantaged workers tend to be clustered.
>
> If the layoff period is reasonably short, the substitution of senior workers for junior workers on layoff enables junior people to "bridge" the layoff period and continue to gain company seniority and job security. If the layoff period is an extended one, and inverse seniority is limited, the application of the concept will at least give junior workers more time to locate jobs outside the company or to fill those job openings inside the company caused by normal attrition.
>
> . . . .
>
> . . . [F]or many disadvantaged workers, securing a job is just the first hurdle; the ability to hold the job is equally critical. Inverse seniority reduces the tendency of cyclical hiring and layoff practices to perpetuate unemployment among this portion of the work force.[188]

The advantages of any program of inverse seniority, which are discussed in detail by Lund, Bumstead and Friedman, are quite obvious. The real difficulty with this proposal is the problem of getting high seniority persons to elect layoff status during a period of economic recession. Most workers on layoff will be receiving less (from SUB and unemployment benefits) than they would receive if they were working full time; thus, there is no real incentive for high senior employees to volunteer to go on layoff status. This is particularly true during a period of economic recession when employees are usually unable to

---

187.   Lund, Bumstead & Friedman, *Inverse Seniority: Timely Answer to the Layoff Dilemma?*, 53 HARV. BUS. REV. 65 (1975) [hereinafter cited as Lund, Bumstead & Friedman].
188.   *Id.* at 66.

accumulate excess funds by working overtime or by "moonlighting." Thus, it is hard to believe that most high seniority workers would be inclined to elect layoff in lieu of full employment in a period of economic recession. In addition, Lund, Bumstead and Friedman properly recognize that any effective program of inverse seniority would be tremendously expensive and, therefore, it is unlikely that many employers will voluntarily initiate such programs.

Probably the most significant suggestions made by Lund, Bumstead and Friedman have to do with proposed government incentives to promote minority employment:

> In the area of direct incentives, several modifications to unemployment insurance regulations might be made. For instance, senior workers on voluntary layoff might be permitted to receive unemployment compensation when they are being replaced by junior people who would otherwise have been laid off from work.
>
> Some states now offer direct financial incentives to companies that provide continuous employment for disadvantaged people coming from public assistance rolls, occupational training programs, and the like. These incentives might be modified to specifically promote [the inverse seniority] approach.
>
> Another direct incentive might be to make compensation received while on inverse seniority layoff exempt from federal income tax, thereby reducing the cost to the company without cutting the amount of take-home pay available to the person on layoff.
>
> Indirect government encouragement of inverse seniority systems might take several forms. One approach would be to finance studies of the detailed mechanism of inverse seniority and economic appraisals of the most promising plans.
>
> [Some] federal agencies have already made rulings favorable to inverse seniority by exempting layoff compensation from minimum wage rules, from unemployment taxes, and from FICA taxes, and by agreeing that employer contributions to an inverse seniority fund are a deductible expense for tax purposes.[189]

Without such formal government support, it seems unlikely that inverse seniority plans will flourish to protect minority employment during periods of economic recession.

C. Work Sharing

A number of persons have suggested "work sharing" plans as possible solutions to the problem of last hired, first fired.[190] Work sharing is a simple concept whereby a company, faced with a need to cut back operations, uniformly reduces the hours of work of all employees

---

189. *Id.* at 72.
190. Blumrosen & Blumrosen, *Layoff or Work Sharing: The Civil Rights Act of 1964 in the Recession of 1975*, in 1 EMPLOYEE RELATIONS L.J. 2 (1975).

so that all may share in the available remaining job opportunities. In other words, work sharing allows all employees to work part time rather than some being laid off while others work full time.

The most obvious difficulty with work sharing is that it runs directly counter to the seniority principle. In those cases where a company has adopted the principle of last hired, first fired, pursuant to a collective bargaining agreement or by long-standing practice, the seniority principle will probably prevail in accordance with the legal precedent established by the *Watkins* case and like decisions. If the rule of *Watkins* is followed, it is simply unlikely that the courts will compel employers to abandon last hired, first fired seniority plans in favor of work sharing.

Another obvious difficulty with work sharing is that it may have at best only limited applicability. For example, if most blacks in a given employment situation are concentrated in certain job categories in the areas where the company intends to reduce its operation and if the minority employees do not have the necessary skills to transfer to other available work, then there may not be much work to share. In addition, the concept of work sharing at least implicitly assumes that a company can uniformly reduce operations so that all of the remaining work can be evenly distributed among the entire work force; but this simply is not a valid assumption in many employment situations. It does not follow that because a company reduces overall production by a certain percentage amount that the manpower needs of the company in its various departments will be reduced by this same percentage amount; as a matter of fact, different parts of the company operation may be reduced by different percentage amounts, depending upon the extent of automation, customer demands, etc.

Furthermore, it must be recognized that, while certain jobs may be maintainable on a full-time basis, many jobs may be available only on a part-time and sporadic basis during a period of economic recession. Any company that has a mix of both of these types of jobs will be hard pressed to share the work among all of the workers. In such a case, the problem of transferability of skills among workers becomes a crucial consideration; this is so because the company will obviously desire to retain only those persons who are capable of performing the work available to be done, whether it be on a full-time or part-time basis. However, to the extent that the available pool of workers share common job skills (for example, police officers), the easier it will be for an employer to share the available work among all of the employees.

One final problem may be raised in connection with work sharing plans. In some cases, the amount of work may be so small that the average income level for each worker may be barely equal to or less than the amount that the same workers would receive in unemployment compensation. Obviously, if such is the case, it makes little sense to maintain all of the workers at a subsistence level of income when some could be earning a full income and others could be receiving the same amount in the form of unemployment compensation.

D. Public Works Jobs

One of the obvious solutions to the problem of unemployment during an economic recession is to create public works jobs of the type created to combat the severe depression of the 1930's. While such a solution may serve to give jobs and income to many disadvantaged persons in society, it is at best a modest, stop-gap measure. Public works jobs usually employ persons in very low skilled jobs and, as a consequence, little or no useful job training is achieved. In addition, public works jobs mostly maintain disadvantaged persons at a subsistence level which is hardly enough to significantly improve the economic status of blacks in this country. In short, public works programs may represent an important remedy in a period of severe economic depression; however, these programs cannot be viewed as a legitimate remedy for race discrimination in employment.

IX. THE REAL COST OF EQUALITY

A number of other solutions have been suggested to the problem of last hired, first fired, but little would be gained by reciting these various proposals here. The cost of equality seemingly involves much more than finding a solution to the problem of last hired, first fired. The current recession has indeed served to highlight the problem of employment discrimination against blacks, but this problem has been with us for nearly 200 years now and it will still be with us when this recession ends. The real challenge, therefore, is to find some workable solutions to the larger issue—that is, the issue of race discrimination.

Last hired, first fired may be but a small symptom of the larger problem. As a consequence, the importance of fictional seniority has conceivably been overstated. Fictional seniority may cure a portion of the problem of racial discrimination, but the gains likely to be achieved might be too insignificant and the costs in terms of white backlash could be too great. Using fictional seniority to remedy race discrimination in employment might be like prescribing an aspirin to cure a headache associated with a gun shot wound. The patient may be temporarily cured of the headache but he may later die from the wound.

Since the evidence is unclear with respect to how much of a detrimental impact last hired, first fired seniority systems have had on minority employment during the 1973-75 recession, one may seriously question the legitimacy of fictional seniority as a remedy for race discrimination in employment. So long as these data remain inconclusive, the competing equities must be given weighty consideration before we resort to fictional seniority which has the effect of displacing white workers with black workers. Among the competing equities, there are at least three important factors that warrant mention. First, any remedy that avoids job displacement along racial lines is clearly preferable to one that has this effect. Second, although seniority systems are not infallible, it must be recalled that the seniority principle has served the interests of large segments of the working class in this country and has protected many employees from arbitrary employer actions for many years. Thus, any attack on seniority systems must consider the consequential losses to all employees (versus employers) stemming from an erosion of the seniority principle. Finally, it must also be recognized that there is no clear legislative policy supporting fictional seniority which results in direct job displacement along racial lines. Given this, the courts will probably continue to be reluctant to compel the use of such a remedy.

However, there is another side to the problem. If it can be conclusively shown that last hired, first fired seniority systems do in fact have a serious detrimental impact on minority employment, then we must be prepared to consider fictional seniority as a remedy to protect blacks who might otherwise be disproportionately disadvantaged during periods of economic recession. It is true that whites may be displaced by the use of fictional seniority remedies, but it is also more likely that the political leaders in our society will react quickly to find solutions to unemployment if a large segment of the white population is forced to suffer without jobs for too long a period of time. White people in the United States have been able to live with high unemployment because unemployment is primarily a black problem. If more nonminority persons had to suffer with blacks and with the problem of unemployment, the problem might be viewed as a matter of national concern worthy of some serious remedial actions. Furthermore, and more importantly, it must be realized that it is possible that minority persons will always be destined to suffer devastating setbacks during periods of economic recession until they get a real foothold in the employment market in the country. It may be that we will find that fictional seniority is one of the few remedies that will truly help blacks to make meaningful gains in employment.

These considerations aside, I would stress that the thing that is most troublesome about the current debates over last hired, first fired and fictional seniority is that these controversies have obscured the really serious issue of race discrimination in employment. This same point was made 10 years ago by Robert L. Carter in *Equality*,[191] when he offered the following significant observations:

> My real objection to the discussion of these concepts in the context of American race relations is that one is engaged in an in-

---

191. R. CARTER, EQUALITY (1965).

teresting but abstract intellectual exercise. What reason is there to debate the legality or wisdom of preferential treatment, when we are not even close to winning the war against discrimination? . . . What we must concentrate on is the elimination of discrimination—only then may discussion about preferences become pertinent to the question of equal treatment.

More dangerously, debate about the wisdom of compensation, preferences, and even benign quotas, insofar as Negroes are concerned, distorts and obscures the basic problem that our society now faces and must resolve. Ours is a racist social order; despite our supposed dedication to the principle of equality without reference to race, color, or previous condition, the white skin is regarded as inherently superior and the black skin as innately inferior. . . .

Today, newspapers are concentrating on what is called the "white backlash" in reaction to the "Negro revolution." In short, the inference from use of this terminology is that Negro progress has been so phenomenal that white people are beginning to react against it. The real facts are that the so-called Negro revolution is merely a drastic break with the traditional Negro image. No great improvements in the Negro's status have yet been accomplished. . . . As the Negro's protest has grown more militant, with resort to direct action, whites, who previously had no need to manifest their prejudices in public, have begun to do so. Since Negroes have become bolder in demanding the removal of all vestiges of slavery, which have kept them shackled in subjugation, whites have become bolder in insisting that the fetters not be removed. All that has happened is that Negroes and whites are being more open and candid in revealing their true sentiments.

I put the discussion of quota, preference and compensatory treatment in the same myth-maintaining category. If we debate about these questions, we can pretend that the problem of discrimination itself has been solved.[192]

As Carter suggests, race discrimination was a problem in 1965, and it remains an unsolved issue in 1975. If change is to come, we must begin to grapple with some of the more fundamental causes and effects of race discrimination in employment. For example, a major problem remains in the areas of white collar, management level, professional and technical jobs. Blacks have been historically excluded from these positions and the attendant economic and social consequences of these exclusionary patterns have been quite severe. Although these facts are well known, very few effective remedies have been developed to cure the problem of employment discrimination in these higher level jobs. It is unlikely that we will be able to train older minority persons to fill many of these white collar, professional and technical jobs in any significant numbers at any time in the near future. Thus, a serious

---

192. *Id.* at 103-05.

commitment must be made to prepare younger minority persons to assume some of these jobs.

If our energies and resources are to be spent on the younger generation of minority persons, we cannot expect these persons to achieve with the same measure of success that older white employees have attained after years of experience.   Blacks entering new jobs must be given time to gain maturity and experience on these jobs; they will need real support from the existing power structures—support that has often been absent in the past; and they will need adequate, not grudging and minimal, training opportunities.   The level of tolerance for mistakes by blacks on the job is often very low.   Mistakes by whites are frequently attributed to immaturity or inexperience; mistakes by blacks are often attributed to incompetence.   These patterns of intolerance simply must be broken if we are ever to achieve a goal of equal employment opportunity.

In addition to these considerations, we also must give some serious attention to the problems of education and unemployment in our society.   In asking the question about the legitimacy of fictional seniority as a remedy to cure last hired, first fired, we implicitly accept the condition of mass unemployment.   Surely it may be asked whether this country should ever tolerate the high levels of unemployment that we have been willing to accept as a consequence of cyclical recessions during the past two decades.   With respect to the problem of education, it may be questioned why we have allowed our public school systems to deteriorate to a point where many parents, both black and white, are looking to private schools to provide adequate educational opportunities for their children.   We may also ask why our public educational school systems do not provide equal educational opportunities for all children and why certain children, living in wealthier neighborhoods, are advantaged.

It is obvious that answers to these questions and solutions to these problems will serve to improve the economic status of blacks in the United States.   However, it is also obvious that solutions to these problems will serve the needs of white persons as well.

It is difficult to examine the long-standing patterns of race discrimination in this country with an intellectual detachment and objectivity. It is all too easy to be enveloped by attitudes of frustration, hostility or cynicism.   However, I am inclined to believe that most human beings live best with hope, not despair; that most of us prefer goodness and not vengeance; and that most people strive to find basic ideals for survival. It may be considered to be somewhat of a luxury to search for ideals during the time in which we live; however, without such a search, we may be doomed to live forever with the inhumanity of racism.

James Comer, in *Beyond Black and White*,[193] proposed certain

---

193.   J. COMER, BEYOND BLACK AND WHITE (1971).

ideals that may provide a foundation for the solutions to the problem of race discrimination. Because Comer's ideas so perfectly summarize the underlying thesis of this author, they are offered here as a fitting conclusion to this paper:

To bring about the kind of change that will reduce Black and White conflict and take America successfully to and through the twenty-first century, a powerful humanist coalition must emerge— a coalition composed of education and health lobbies, consumer advocates, environmentalists, minorities, women, the young, liberals and humanistic conservatives. Political and social action— in integrated groups, in separate groups, in temporary and sustained coalition—is needed to force the leaders of the country to respond realistically to the needs of all its citizens. . . .

We have now reached the danger point. We do not have the social programs which take the extreme fear and insecurity out of modern living. The people who have been scapegoated are angry. More fortunate but still relatively powerless Whites are frustrated, confused and feeling falsely blamed. The level of trust between various interest groups in America is extremely low. Many leaders still view political victory or economic gain by any means necessary as more honorable and American than supporting essential social policies that may lead to political defeat or less immediate financial profit. . . .

National leaders must reconcile their own needs and desires and those of their class with the needs of all the people, the environment and the society. . . .

The specific programs needed are no mystery. New housing, health care, job and income guarantees, child-care and retraining programs are but a few of them. Without a leadership group or national ego committed to creating a national sense of community, new programs can continue to divide blacks and whites, rich and poor, old and young, women and men, while benefitting only a few—relieving the insecurity of only a few. The humanist coalition everywhere in America must make certain that all our new social programs are designed to reduce the level of fear, anxiety and insecurity of all America.

AUTHOR'S NOTE

On March 24, 1976, the Supreme Court decided *Franks v. Bowman Transportation Co.*, 96 S.Ct. 1251 (1976), and ruled that retroactive seniority must be given to identifiable victims of discrimination under Title VII.

Although *Franks* has been described by some as a landmark decision, it is hardly worthy of such acclaim. Notwithstanding the fact that the Court decided *Franks* by a bare 5-3 majority, the judgment in the case was plainly justified and surely not surprising. In 1975 the Court had made it clear in *Albemarle Paper Co. v. Moody* that the remedial provisions of Title VII were fashioned after the remedial provisions of the National Labor Relations Act and should therefore be construed in a manner consistent with the case precedent under the NLRA. Reinstatement with back pay and with retroactive seniority rights is a common remedy for victims of unfair labor practices under the NLRA in both unlawful discharge and refusal to hire cases. Thus in following the view that had been expressed in *Albemarle*, the Supreme Court could easily rule in *Franks* (as it did) that persons who have been unlawfully denied job rights at the *hiring* stage of employment should be awarded both back pay and retroactive seniority under Title VII.

The decision in *Franks* may significantly affect the resolution of two related situations in which seniority relief may be sought. First, there is the situation where an employer's reputation for discriminatory hiring practices is so widespread that minority persons can show they were discouraged even from applying for a job; the question in such a case will be whether such "discouraged applicants" should be given retroactive seniority along with those persons who actually applied for jobs and were rejected by the employer. Second, there is the situation where a minority person can only show that the employer was guilty of past discrimination but cannot show that he or she was personally either refused employment or discouraged from applying. In dealing with these two situations the significance of *Franks* is for now lost in the battle, between Justice Brennan writing for the majority and Justices Powell and Rehnquist and Chief Justice Burger dissenting in part, over the weight to be accorded to the interests and expectations of white male employees (with vested seniority rights) in determining the appropriateness of seniority relief for minority (and women) applicants.

The Court in *Franks* granted seniority relief to identifiable victims of prior discriminatory hiring practices on the basis of an assumption "that a sharing of the burden of the past discrimination is presumptively necessary." Considering the facts of the *Franks* case, the Court found it relatively easy to answer Chief Justice Burger's assertion that such an assumption resulted in "robbing Peter to pay Paul." Rather than viewing the white employee as an "innocent . . . 'holder-in-due-course' . . . without notice of any defect," the majority in *Franks* seemed to view such white employees more like receivers of stolen goods, that is, persons who probably would not have obtained their jobs but for the past illegal discrimination. As such, the white employees had no legitimate claim to superior seniority standing over identifiable victims of past unlawful discrimination.

The Court also noted that white employees would not be deprived of earned seniority status by virtue of retroactive seniority given to identifiable victims of discrimination. The black plaintiffs in *Franks* were not asking for elimination of the existing seniority system, "but only an award of the seniority status they would have individually enjoyed under the [existing seniority] system but for the illegal discriminatory refusal to hire."

But even with such an award of retroactive seniority, the black plaintiffs in *Franks* still remained relatively subordinated in the course of future upward or downward job movements to those white employees who had been hired in their stead because of the past discrimination. The significance of the relief granted in *Franks* is also further diminished by the fact that relatively few minority persons or women are likely to benefit from grants of retroactive seniority. In *Franks*, for example, out of 166 minority employees who had at one time or another been rejected by the company only about seven later applied and were hired pursuant to the district court order.

Probably the most significant and depressing thing about the *Franks* decisions is that the Court split 5-3 on what should have been a simple and unanimous decision. Such a split may portend an unfavorable resolution of the case involving minority persons who are discouraged from applying for jobs because of the employer's reputation for discrimination. On this point, there are at least two major hurdles of proof in cases involving persons who are discouraged from applying. First, there will be no employment application date to provide a convenient reference point for back pay and retroactive seniority determinations. Second, the image of aggressiveness conjured up by the work ethic will always leave nagging doubts for some that the alleged victim of discrimination was really avoiding work rather than being discouraged from applying.

One possible answer might be to adjust the burden of proof in these cases. Plaintiffs who allege that an employer's reputation discouraged them from applying for a job could be required to produce evidence that they were actively looking for work at a time when the employer or union were in fact guilty of past discrimination and that the employer's discriminatory hiring practices were generally well known by minority persons within the applicable labor market. The employer could then point to past recruitment and hiring practices to dispel the claim of discrimination and/or to dispel the charge that minority persons had been "discouraged" from applying for jobs. This could be done by a showing that minority persons were in fact recruited; that minority persons consistently applied for jobs (and therefore could not have been "discouraged"); and that more than a token number of minority persons were hired. However, the employer should not be able to rebut such a charge of discrimination by merely showing that a large number of minority persons had applied for jobs in the past if none were ever hired.

Once plaintiffs have met the burden of establishing that they were in fact "discouraged" from applying for jobs because of the employer's reputation, the equitable considerations should be no different than those cited by the Court in *Franks*.

The more difficult problems in the so-called retroactive fictional seniority cases arise when a company finally starts hiring blacks and none of the minority persons hired are specific discriminatees. In such cases, if the employer subsequently finds it necessary to cut back the work force, and fictional seniority is granted to the recently hired minority persons, white employees who had an expectation of continued employment or promotion based on their seniority will be denied their expectations because of their race. However, if the remedy is denied, a round of layoffs can restore the earlier imbalance among minority employees.

The Court in *Franks* indicated that where an individual has been personally discriminated against, sharing the burden of such discrimination will be presumptively necessary in order to assure access to future job movement. The Court indicated that Title VII does not bar otherwise appropriate relief once an illegal discriminatory practice occurring after the effective date of the Act is proved. But the situations when seniority relief is appropriate may be limited to those cases where the plaintiffs can identify themselves as persons who would have had that seniority but for the illegal discrimination. There is nothing in the *Franks* decision to indicate that the Court might likely approve "fictional seniority" in some later cases arising under Title VII.

Justice Powell, in his dissent in *Franks*, noted that seniority status determines an employee's preferential rights to various economic advantages. A request of competitive seniority for an individual who cannot be identified as a victim of prior discrimination may run head-long into the charge that the only basis for such a request is that the individual's race or sex is somehow underrepresented in the employer's work force. That request may therefore be barred by the Title VII prohibition of preferential treatment merely to restore statistical imbalances. The fact that the majority in *Franks* did not answer Justice Powell's concern may indicate the Court's unwillingness to take this last step. Instead, the Court might rely on other remedies such as "front pay" awards or injunctive "hold-harmless" remedies in layoff situations (both of which were cited by the Court in footnote 38), where the impact on arguably innocent white employees is minimal and the offending employer or union bears the brunt.

The reference to front pay, in footnote 38 of the majority opinion and in Chief Justice Burger's dissenting opinion, raises some interesting possibilities for the future. Although the majority opinion failed to decide the question, the reference to front pay suggests that the Court might consider the use of this remedial device in "fictional seniority" cases involving no identifiable discriminatees. The use of front pay instead of fictional seniority would clearly be more than UAW officials had in mind when they suggested this remedy; the UAW proposal limited the front pay remedy to situations involving identifiable discriminatees.

One of the most surprising things about the *Franks* decision is Chief Justice Burger's dissenting opinion in which he cites "front pay" as a preferable remedial alternative to seniority relief. Chief Justice Burger seems to believe that the seniority relief is inequitable because it is likely to result in the displacement of white workers by black victims of past discrimination. However, he obviously fails to understand the full impact of a front pay remedy. Front pay, just like retroactive seniority, will result in some job displacement of white employees; this is so because if a company must pay black workers who have been laid off (pursuant to a front pay remedy), it will very likely lay off more senior white workers than would otherwise have been necessary in order to achieve the dollar savings contemplated by the layoff. It is true that this is merely an indirect form of job displacement, but it is no less significant than the job displacement which occurs as a consequence of a grant of retroactive seniority.

The real significance of *Franks* is difficult to measure. The slim majority in *Franks*, on such a simple issue, is hardly an encouraging sign. If *Franks* is read in conjunction with a case like *Washington v. Davis*, 44 L.W. 4789 (June 8, 1976), it may portend a gloomy future for victims of employment discrimination. On the positive side, *Franks* does at least indicate that there are five members of the Court who still understand and are willing to enforce the proscription against discrimination under Title VII.

BIBLIOGRAPHY

Beale, Howard K. "On Rewriting Reconstruction History." *American Historical Review*, 45 (1940), 802-27.

Blumrosen, Alfred W., and Blumrosen, Ruth G. "Layoffs or Work Sharing: The Civil Rights Act of 1964 in the Recession of 1975." *Employee Relations Law Journal*, 1 (1975), 2-25.

Brimmer, Andrew F. "The Negro in the National Economy." In *The American Negro Reference Book*, edited by John P. Davis. Englewood Cliffs, N.J.: Prentice-Hall, 1966.

Cable, George W. *The Negro Question: A Selection of Writings on Civil Rights in the South.* Edited by Arlin Turner. Garden City, N.J.: Doubleday, 1958.

Carter, Robert L.; Kenyon, Dorothy; Marcuse, Peter; and Miller, Loren. *Equality.* New York: Pantheon Books, 1965.

Civil Rights Act of 1964. Washington, D.C.: Bureau of National Affairs, 1964.

Comer, James. *Beyond Black and White.* New York: Quadrangle Books, 1971.

David, Jay. *Growing Up Black.* New York: William Morrow, 1968.

Davie, Maurice R. *Negroes in American Society.* New York: McGraw-Hill, 1949.

Davis, John P., ed. *The American Negro Reference Book.* Englewood Cliffs, N.J.: Prentice-Hall, 1966.

Du Bois, W. E. B. *Black Reconstruction: An Essay toward a History of the Part Which Black Folk Played in an Attempt to Reconstruct Democracy, 1860-1888.* New York: Russell & Russell, 1935.

―――. "Three Centuries of Discrimination." *The Crisis*, 54, no. 12 (Dec., 1947), 362-64, 379-81.

Edwards, Harry T. "Substantive Legal Developments under Title VII." *Law Quadrangle Notes*, 19, no. 2 (Winter, 1975), 10-19.

Edwards, Harry T., and Zaretsky, Barry L. "Preferential Remedies for Employment Discrimination." *Michigan Law Review*, 74 (Nov., 1975), 1-47.

Ellison, Ralph, *Invisible Man.* New York: Random House, 1947.

Equal Employment Opportunity Act of 1972. Washington, D.C.: Bureau of National Affairs, 1973.

Farley, Reynolds, and Hermalin, Albert. "The 1960's: A Decade of Progress for Blacks?" In *Racial Discrimination in the United States*, edited by Thomas F. Pettigrew. New York: Harper and Row, 1975.

Fein, Rashi. "An Economic and Social Profile of the Negro American." *Daedalus*, 94 (Fall, 1965), 815-46.

Franklin, John Hope. *From Slavery to Freedom: A History of American Negroes.* 4th ed. New York: Alfred A. Knopf, 1974.

Friedman, Alan V., and Katz, Allen M. "Retroactive Seniority for the Identifiable Victim under Title VII—Must Last Hired First Fired Give Way?" In *Proceedings of the New York University Twenty-Eighth Annual Conference on Labor*, edited by Richard Adelman. New York: Matthew Bender, 1976.

Ginzberg, Eli, and Hiestand, Dale L. "Employment Patterns of Negro Men and Women." In *The American Negro Reference Book*, edited by John P. Davis. Englewood Cliffs, N.J.: Prentice-Hall, 1966.

Glenn, Norval D. "Some Changes in the Relative Status of American Nonwhites, 1940 to 1960." *Phylon*, 24, no. 2 (Summer, 1963), 109-22.

―――. "Change in the Social and Economic Conditions of Black Americans during the 1960's." In *Blacks in the United States*, edited by Glenn D. Norval and Charles M. Bonjean. San Francisco: Chandler Publishing, 1969.

―――. "The Occupations and Income of Black Americans." In *Blacks in the United States*, edited by Norval D. Glenn and Charles M. Bonjean. San Francisco: Chandler Publishing, 1969.

————, and Bonjean, Charles M., eds. *Blacks in the United States.* San Francisco: Chandler Publishing, 1969.

Goldschmid, M. L. *Black Americans and White Racism: Theory and Research.* New York: Holt, Rinehart and Winston, 1970.

Greenberg, Jack. *Race Relations and American Law.* New York: Columbia University Press, 1959.

Henderson, Vivian W. "Region, Race, and Jobs." In *Employment, Race, and Poverty,* edited by Arthur M. Ross and Herbert Hill. New York: Harcourt, Brace and World, 1967.

Hiestand, Dale L. *Discrimination in Employment: An Appraisal of the Research.* Policy Papers in Human Resources and Industrial Relations, no. 16. Ann Arbor: University of Michigan, Institute of Labor and Industrial Relations, 1970.

Jacobson, Julius, ed. *The Negro and the American Labor Movement.* New York: Doubleday, 1968.

Killingsworth, Charles C. *Jobs and Income for Negroes.* Policy Papers in Human Resources and Industrial Relations, no. 6. Ann Arbor: University of Michigan, Institute of Labor and Industrial Relations, 1968.

————. "Negroes in a Changing Labor Market." In *Employment, Race, and Poverty,* edited by Arthur M. Ross and Herbert Hill. New York: Harcourt, Brace and World, 1967.

Larson, E. Richard. "The Development of Section 1981 as a Remedy for Racial Discrimination in Private Employment." *Harvard Civil Rights-Civil Liberties Law Review,* 7 (1972), 56-102.

"Last Hired, First Fired Layoffs and Title VII." Note, *Harvard Law Review,* 88 (May, 1975), 1544-70.

Lieberson, Stanley, and Fuguitt, Glenn V. "Negro-White Occupational Differences in the Absence of Discrimination." In *Racial Discrimination in the United States,* edited by Thomas F. Pettigrew. New York: Harper and Row, 1975.

Lomax, Louis E. *The Negro Revolt.* New York: Harper and Row, 1962.

Lund, Robert T.: Bumstead, Dennis C.; and Friedman, Sheldon. "Inverse Seniority: Timely Answer to the Layoff Dilemma?" *Harvard Business Review,* 53 (Sept.-Oct., 1975), 65-72.

Mack, Raymond W., ed. *Race, Class, and Power.* 2nd ed. New York: Van Nostrand Reinhold, 1968.

Mayhew, Leon. *Law and Equal Opportunity: A Study of the Massachusetts Commission against Discrimination.* Joint Center for Urban Studies Publication Series. Cambridge, Mass.: Harvard University Press, 1968.

Meier, August, and Rudwick, Elliott M., eds. *The Making of Black America: Essays in Negro Life and History.* Studies in American Negro Life Series. New York: Atheneum, 1969.

Mendelson, Wallace. *Discrimination.* Englewood Cliffs, N.J.: Prentice-Hall, 1962.

Miller, Elizabeth W., ed. *The Negro in America: A Bibliography.* Cambridge, Mass.: Harvard University Press, 1966.

————, and Fisher, Mary, eds. *The Negro in America: A Bibliography.* Revised ed. Cambridge, Mass.: Harvard University Press, 1970.

Myrdal, Gunnar, with the assistance of Richard Sterner and Arnold Rose. *An American Dilemma: The Negro Problem and Modern Democracy.* New York: Harper and Row, 1944.

————. *Challenge to Affluence.* New York: Pantheon Books, 1963.

National Urban League. *Full Employment as a National Goal: Proceedings of the 64th National Urban League Conference, San Francisco, California, July 28-31, 1974.* New York: National Urban League, 1975.

National Urban League Research Department. *Black Families in the 1974-75 Depression.* Washington, D.C.: National Urban League, 1975.

————. "Quarterly Economic Report on the Black Worker." Fourth Quarter, 1974. Washington, D.C.: National Urban League, 1975.

————. "Quarterly Economic Report on the Black Worker." First Quarter, 1975. Washington, D.C.: National Urban League, 1975.

————. "Quarterly Economic Report on the Black Worker." Second Quarter, 1975. Washington, D.C.: National Urban League, 1975.

New York Times. "Last Hired, and Usually the First Let Go." Jan. 29, 1975, p. 17.

————. "Recession Layoffs and the Civil Rights of Minorities." Jan. 29, 1975, p. 17.

————. "Minorities and Women Fearing Trauma." Jan. 5, 1975, pp. III-30, 31.

Northrup, Herbert R., and Rowan, Richard L. *The Negro and Employment Opportunity: Problems and Practices.* Ann Arbor: Bureau of Industrial Relations, Graduate School of Business Administration, University of Michigan, 1965.

Pettigrew, Thomas F. *A Profile of the Negro American.* New York: Van Nostrand Reinhold, 1964.

————. *Racially Separate or Together?* New York: McGraw-Hill, 1971.

————, ed. *Racial Discrimination in the United States.* New York: Harper and Row, 1975.

Rawick, George P. *The American Slave: A Composite Autobiography,* Pt. 1, Pt. 2. Contributions in Afro-American and African Studies, no. 2. New York: Green wood, 1972.

Rose, Arnold. *The Negro in America.* New York: Harper, 1948.

————, ed. *Race Prejudice and Discrimination: Readings in Intergroup Relations in the United States.* New York: Alfred A. Knopf, 1951.

Ross, Arthur M. "The Negro in the American Economy." In *Employment, Race, and Poverty,* edited by Arthur M. Ross and Herbert Hill. New York: Harcourt, Brace and World, 1967.

————, and Hill, Herbert, eds. *Employment, Race, and Poverty.* New York: Harcourt, Brace and World, 1967.

Silberman, Charles E. *Crisis in Black and White.* New York: Random House, 1964.

Simkins, Francis B. "New Viewpoints of Southern Reconstruction." *Journal of Southern History,* 5 (1939), 49-61.

Spero, Sterling D., and Harris, Abram L. *The Black Worker: The Negro and the Labor Market.* New York: Columbia University Press, 1931.

Taft, Philip. *Organized Labor in American History.* New York: Harper and Row, 1964.

Twombly, Robert C., ed. *Blacks in White America since 1865: Issues and Interpretations.* New York: McKay, 1971.

U.S. Bureau of the Census. *Metropolitan Area Statistics.* Reprinted from *Statistical Abstract of the United States, 1971.* 1971.

————. *The Social and Economic Status of the Black Population in the United States, 1973.* Current Population Reports, Special Studies, Series P-23, No. 48. Washington, D.C.: Government Printing Office. 1974.

————. *The Social and Economic Status of the Black Population in the United States, 1974.* Current Population Reports, Special Studies, Series P-23, No. 54. Washington, D.C.: Government Printing Office. 1975.

U.S. Commission on Civil Rights. *Civil Rights '63: 1963 Report of the United States Commission on Civil Rights.* 1963.

U.S. Department of Labor, Bureau of Labor Statistics. *Handbook of Labor Statistics, 1971.* Bulletin 1705. 1971.

————. *Handbook of Labor Statistics, 1974.* Bulletin 1825. 1974.

————. "Current Labor Statistics." *Monthly Labor Review,* 98, no. 9 (Sept., 1975), 77-115.

Van Den Berghe, P. L. *Race and Racism: A Comparative Perspective.* New York: John Wiley and Sons, 1967.

VanDer Zanden, James W. *American Minority Relations: The Sociology of Race and Ethnic Groups.* 3rd ed. New York: Ronald Press, 1972.

Wade, Richard C. *Slavery in the Cities: The South 1820-1860.* New York: Oxford University Press, 1964.

Wall Street Journal. "Courts' Protection against Job Layoffs Sought by Minorities." Nov. 5, 1974, pp. 1, 27.

Washington Post. "Black Joblessness Put at 26%." July 29, 1975, p. A2.

———. "Error Is Corrected in Layoffs Report." April 29, 1975, p. A2.

———. "White Males Hit by Layoffs." April 24, 1975, pp. A1, A16.

Weaver, Robert C. "Negro Labor since 1929." In *Race Prejudice and Discrimination: Readings in Intergroup Relations in the United States*, edited by Arnold Rose. New York: Alfred A. Knopf, 1951.

APPENDIX

TABLES OF EMPLOYMENT STATISTICS

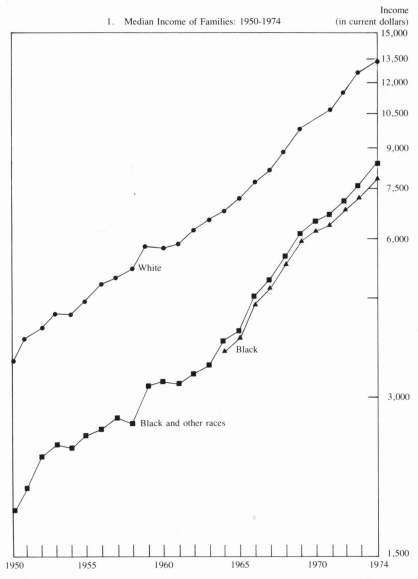

1.   Median Income of Families: 1950-1974

Income
(in current dollars)

SOURCE: U.S. Bureau of the Census, *The Social and Economic Status of the Black Population in the United States, 1974,* Current Population Reports, Special Studies, Series P-23, No. 54, p. 21.

2. Median Income of Families: 1950-1974

(In current dollars)

Year	Race of head			Ratio: Black and other races to white	Ratio: Black to white
	Black and other races	Black	White		
1950............................	$ 1,869	(NA)	$ 3,445	0.54	(NA)
1951............................	2,032	(NA)	3,859	0.53	(NA)
1952............................	2,338	(NA)	4,114	0.57	(NA)
1953............................	2,461	(NA)	4,392	0.56	(NA)
1954............................	2,410	(NA)	4,339	0.56	(NA)
1955............................	2,549	(NA)	4,605	0.55	(NA)
1956............................	2,628	(NA)	4,993	0.53	(NA)
1957............................	2,764	(NA)	5,166	0.54	(NA)
1958............................	2,711	(NA)	5,300	0.51	(NA)
1959............................	3,161	$ 3,047	5,893	0.54	0.52
1960............................	3,233	(NA)	5,835	0.55	(NA)
1961............................	3,191	(NA)	5,981	0.53	(NA)
1962............................	3,330	(NA)	6,237	0.53	(NA)
1963............................	3,465	(NA)	6,548	0.53	(NA)
1964............................	3,839	3,724	6,858	0.56	0.54
1965............................	3,994	3,886	7,251	0.55	0.54
1966............................	4,674	4,507	7,792	0.60	0.58
1967[1]	5,094	4,875	8,234	0.62	0.59
1968............................	5,590	5,360	8,937	0.63	0.60
1969............................	6,191	5,999	9,794	0.63	0.61
1970............................	6,516	6,279	10,236	0.64	0.61
1971[2]	6,714	6,440	10,672	0.63	0.60
1972[2]	7,106	6,864	11,549	0.62	0.59
1973[2]	7,596	7,269	12,595	0.60	0.58
1974[2]					
United States...............	8,265	7,808	13,356	0.62	0.58
South......................	6,805	6,730	12,050	0.56	0.56
North and West.........	10,039	9,271	13,906	0.72	0.67
Northeast	9,399	8,788	14,164	0.66	0.62
North Central	9,901	9,846	14,017	0.71	0.70
West...................	11,107	8,585	13,339	0.83	0.64

Note: Income figures for 1974 from the Current Population Survey conducted in March 1975, which recently became available, have been included in most of the tables in this section. A few of the tables in this section show income data for the year 1973. Data for 1959 are from the 1960 census; figures for the remaining years are from Current Population Surveys.

NA Not available. The ratio of black to white median family income first became available from this survey in 1964.

[1] Revised, based on processing correction.

[2] Based on 1970 census population controls; therefore, not strictly comparable to data for earlier years.

SOURCE: U.S. Bureau of the Census, *The Social and Economic Status of the Black Population in the United States, 1974,* Current Population Reports, Special Studies, Series P-23, No. 54, p. 25.

3. Median Income of Families, by Type of Family and Labor Force Status of Wife:
1967 and 1970-1974

(In current dollars)

Type of family and race of head	1967	1970	1971	1972	1973	1974
BLACK						
All families..................	$ 4,875	$ 6,279	$ 6,440	$ 6,864	$ 7,269	$ 7,808
Male head[1]..........................	5,737	7,766	8,067	9,037	9,549	10,365
Married, wife present	5,808	7,816	8,178	9,166	9,729	10,530
Wife in paid labor force	7,272	9,721	10,274	11,336	12,266	12,982
Wife not in paid labor force	4,662	5,961	6,503	6,900	7,148	7,773
Female head........................	3,004	3,576	3,645	3,840	4,226	4,465
WHITE						
All families..................	$ 8,234	$10,236	$10,672	$11,549	$12,595	$13,356
Male head[1]..........................	8,557	10,697	11,143	12,102	13,253	14,055
Married, wife present	8,588	10,723	11,191	12,137	13,297	14,099
Wife in paid labor force	10,196	12,543	13,098	14,148	15,654	16,825
Wife not in paid labor force	7,743	9,531	9,976	10,806	11,716	12,381
Female head........................	4,855	5,754	5,842	6,213	6,560	7,363
RATIO: BLACK TO WHITE						
All families..................	0.59	0.61	0.60	0.59	0.58	0.58
Male head[1]..........................	0.67	0.73	0.72	0.75	0.72	0.74
Married, wife present	0.68	0.73	0.73	0.76	0.73	0.75
Wife in paid labor force	0.71	0.78	0.78	0.80	0.78	0.77
Wife not in paid labor force	0.60	0.63	0.65	0.64	0.61	0.63
Female head........................	0.62	0.62	0.62	0.62	0.64	0.61

[1]   Includes other male heads, not shown separately.

SOURCE: U.S. Bureau of the Census, *The Social and Economic Status of the Black Population in the United States, 1974,* Current Population Reports, Special Studies, Series P-23, No. 54, p. 33.

4. Families below the Low-Income Level, by Sex of Head: 1959 and 1967-1974

(Families as of the following year)

Year	All families		Families with male head		Families with female head	
	Black	White	Black	White	Black	White
	Number (thousands)					
1959.........	1,860	6,027	1,309	5,037	551	990
1967.........	1,555	4,056	839	3,019	716	1,037
1968.........	1,366	3,616	660	2,595	706	1,021
1969[1]	1,366	3,575	629	2,506	737	1,069
1970[1]	1,481	3,708	648	2,606	834	1,102
1971[1]	1,484	3,751	605	2,560	879	1,191
1972[1]	1,529	3,441	558	2,306	972	1,135
1973[1]	1,527	3,219	553	2,029	974	1,190
1974[1]	1,530	3,482	506	2,185	1,024	1,297
	Percent below the low-income level					
1959.........	48.1	14.8	43.3	13.4	65.4	30.0
1967.........	33.9	9.0	25.3	7.4	56.3	25.9
1968.........	29.4	8.0	19.9	6.3	53.2	25.2
1969[1]	27.9	7.7	17.9	6.0	53.3	25.7
1970[1]	29.5	8.0	18.6	6.2	54.3	25.0
1971[1]	28.8	7.9	17.2	5.9	53.5	26.5
1972[1]	29.0	7.1	16.2	5.3	53.3	24.3
1973[1]	28.1	6.6	15.4	4.6	52.7	24.5
1974[1]	27.8	7.0	14.2	4.9	52.8	24.9

[1] Based on 1970 census population controls; therefore, not strictly comparable to data for earlier years.

SOURCE: U.S. Bureau of the Census, *The Social and Economic Status of the Black Population in the United States, 1974*, Current Population Reports, Special Studies, Series P-23, No. 54, p. 43.

5. Unemployed Persons 16 Years and Over and Unemployment Rates, by Sex and Color, 1947-1973

Year and month	Number unemployed (thousands)									Unemployment rate								
	Total			White			Negro and other races			Total			White			Negro and other races		
	Total	Males	Females	Total	Males	Females	Total	Males	Females	Total	Males	Females	Total	Males	Females	Total	Males	Females
1947	2,311	1,692	619	(1)	(1)	(1)	(1)	(1)	(1)	3.9	4.0	3.7	—	—	—	—	—	—
1948	2,276	1,559	717	(1)	(1)	(1)	(1)	(1)	(1)	3.8	3.6	4.1	3.5	3.4	3.8	5.9	5.8	6.1
1949	3,637	2,572	1,065	(1)	(1)	(1)	(1)	(1)	(1)	5.9	5.9	6.0	5.6	5.6	5.7	8.9	9.6	7.9
1950	3,288	2,239	1,049	(1)	(1)	(1)	(1)	(1)	(1)	5.3	5.1	5.7	4.9	4.7	5.3	9.0	9.4	8.4
1951	2,055	1,221	834	(1)	(1)	(1)	(1)	(1)	(1)	3.3	2.8	4.4	3.1	2.6	4.2	5.3	4.9	6.1
1952	1,883	1,185	698	(1)	(1)	(1)	(1)	(1)	(1)	3.0	2.8	3.6	2.8	2.5	3.3	5.4	5.2	5.7
1953	1,834	1,202	632	(1)	(1)	(1)	(1)	(1)	(1)	2.9	2.8	3.3	2.7	2.5	3.1	4.5	4.8	4.1
1954	3,532	2,344	1,188	2,860	1,913	947	674	431	243	5.5	5.3	6.0	5.0	4.8	5.6	9.9	10.3	9.3
1955	2,852	1,854	998	2,248	1,475	773	601	376	225	4.4	4.2	4.9	3.9	3.7	4.3	8.7	8.8	8.4
1956	2,750	1,711	1,039	2,162	1,368	794	592	345	247	4.1	3.8	4.8	3.6	3.4	4.2	8.3	7.9	8.9
1957	2,859	1,841	1,018	2,289	1,478	811	569	363	206	4.3	4.1	4.7	3.8	3.6	4.3	7.9	8.3	7.3
1958	4,602	3,098	1,504	3,679	2,488	1,191	925	611	314	6.8	6.8	6.8	6.1	6.1	6.2	12.6	13.8	10.8
1959	3,740	2,420	1,320	2,947	1,904	1,044	794	518	276	5.5	5.3	5.9	4.8	4.6	5.3	10.7	11.5	9.4
1960	3,852	2,486	1,366	3,063	1,987	1,076	787	497	290	5.5	5.4	5.9	4.9	4.8	5.3	10.2	10.7	9.4
1961	4,714	2,997	1,717	3,742	2,398	1,344	970	599	371	6.7	6.4	7.2	6.0	5.7	6.5	12.4	12.8	11.8
1962	3,911	2,423	1,488	3,052	1,915	1,137	859	508	351	5.5	5.2	6.2	4.9	4.6	5.5	10.9	10.9	11.0
1963	4,070	2,472	1,598	3,208	1,976	1,232	864	496	368	5.7	5.2	6.5	5.0	4.7	5.8	10.8	10.5	11.2
1964	3,786	2,205	1,581	2,999	1,779	1,220	786	426	360	5.2	4.6	6.2	4.6	4.1	5.5	9.6	8.9	10.6
1965	3,366	1,914	1,452	2,691	1,556	1,135	676	359	317	4.5	4.0	5.5	4.1	3.6	5.0	8.1	7.4	9.2
1966	2,875	1,551	1,324	2,253	1,240	1,013	621	311	310	3.8	3.2	4.8	3.3	2.8	4.3	7.3	6.3	8.6
1967	2,975	1,508	1,468	2,338	1,208	1,130	638	299	338	3.8	3.1	5.2	3.4	2.7	4.6	7.4	6.0	9.1
1968	2,817	1,419	1,397	2,226	1,142	1,084	590	277	313	3.6	2.9	4.8	3.2	2.6	4.3	6.7	5.6	8.3
1969	2,831	1,403	1,428	2,261	1,137	1,124	570	266	304	3.5	2.8	4.7	3.1	2.5	4.2	6.4	5.3	7.8
1970	4,088	2,235	1,853	3,337	1,856	1,480	752	379	373	4.9	4.4	5.9	4.5	4.0	5.4	8.2	7.3	9.3
1971	4,993	2,776	2,217	4,074	2,302	1,772	919	474	445	5.9	5.3	6.9	5.4	4.9	6.3	9.9	9.1	10.8
1972	4,840	2,635	2,205	3,884	2,160	1,724	956	475	482	5.6	4.9	6.6	5.0	4.5	5.9	10.0	8.9	11.3
1973	4,304	2,240	2,064	3,411	1,818	1,593	894	423	471	4.9	4.1	6.0	4.3	3.7	5.3	8.9	7.6	10.5

1 Absolute numbers by color are not available prior to 1954 because population controls by color were not introduced into the Current Population Survey until that year.

Year and month	Number unemployed (thousands)			White			Negro and other races			Unemployment rate			White			Negro and other races		
	Total	Males	Fe-males	Total	Males	Fe-males	Total	Males	Fe-males	Total	Males	Fe-males	Total	Males	Fe-males	Total	Males	Fe-males
1972																		
January	5,447	3,240	2,207	4,423	2,713	1,710	1,025	527	498	6.4	6.2	6.8	5.9	5.8	6.0	11.2	10.5	12.0
February	5,412	3,293	2,119	4,383	2,711	1,672	1,028	581	447	6.4	6.3	6.5	5.8	5.8	5.8	11.0	11.2	10.8
March	5,215	3,076	2,189	4,239	2,565	1,674	976	511	465	6.1	5.9	6.5	5.6	5.4	5.8	10.4	9.8	11.1
April	4,697	2,668	2,030	3,859	2,227	1,632	838	440	398	5.5	5.1	6.2	5.1	4.7	5.7	9.0	8.4	9.6
May	4,344	2,390	1,954	3,504	1,942	1,561	840	447	393	5.1	4.5	5.9	4.6	4.1	5.4	8.9	8.5	9.4
June	5,426	2,827	2,599	4,299	2,304	1,995	1,126	523	604	6.2	5.2	7.8	5.5	4.7	6.9	11.3	9.4	13.8
July	5,173	2,659	2,514	4,053	2,095	1,958	1,121	564	556	5.8	4.8	7.5	5.2	4.2	6.7	11.2	10.0	12.7
August	4,857	2,437	2,420	3,894	1,964	1,930	963	473	490	5.5	4.4	7.2	5.0	4.0	6.6	9.7	8.4	11.4
September	4,658	2,239	2,420	3,723	1,835	1,888	935	404	532	5.4	4.2	7.2	4.8	3.8	6.5	9.8	7.6	12.6
October	4,470	2,227	2,243	3,573	1,839	1,733	897	387	510	5.1	4.2	6.6	4.6	3.8	5.9	9.3	7.3	11.9
November	4,266	2,238	2,028	3,368	1,827	1,541	898	411	487	4.9	4.2	6.0	4.4	3.8	5.2	9.3	7.7	11.2
December	4,116	2,328	1,788	3,291	1,903	1,387	825	425	400	4.7	4.4	5.3	4.3	4.0	4.7	8.6	8.0	9.3
1973																		
January	4,675	2,603	2,072	3,835	2,207	1,629	840	397	443	5.5	5.0	6.2	5.0	4.7	5.6	9.0	7.7	10.5
February	4,845	2,713	2,132	3,949	2,281	1,668	895	432	463	5.6	5.1	6.3	5.1	4.8	5.7	9.3	8.2	10.7
March	4,512	2,530	1,981	3,625	2,096	1,529	887	434	453	5.2	4.7	5.8	4.7	4.4	5.2	9.0	8.0	10.2
April	4,174	2,286	1,888	3,316	1,851	1,466	858	435	423	4.8	4.3	5.6	4.3	3.9	4.9	8.7	7.9	9.7
May	3,799	2,052	1,747	3,009	1,645	1,364	790	407	383	4.3	3.8	5.1	3.9	3.4	4.6	8.1	7.4	8.9
June	4,847	2,443	2,404	3,755	1,934	1,821	1,092	509	583	5.4	4.4	6.9	4.7	3.9	6.0	10.7	8.9	12.9
July	4,550	2,288	2,262	3,432	1,742	1,690	1,118	546	572	5.0	4.1	6.5	4.3	3.5	5.6	10.6	9.3	12.2
August	4,208	2,035	2,174	3,301	1,619	1,681	908	416	492	4.7	3.7	6.3	4.1	3.3	5.6	8.8	7.2	10.7
September	4,165	1,900	2,265	3,244	1,521	1,723	921	379	542	4.7	3.5	6.5	4.1	3.1	5.7	9.1	6.8	12.0
October	3,763	1,819	1,945	2,980	1,449	1,531	783	369	414	4.2	3.3	5.5	3.7	3.0	5.0	7.7	6.5	9.2
November	4,056	2,025	2,031	3,206	1,641	1,565	850	384	465	4.5	3.7	5.7	4.0	3.4	5.0	8.3	6.8	10.2
December	4,058	2,191	1,868	3,272	1,824	1,448	786	366	419	4.5	4.0	5.3	4.1	3.7	4.7	7.7	6.5	9.2

SOURCE: U.S. Department of Labor, Bureau of Labor Statistics, *Handbook of Labor Statistics, 1974*, Bulletin 1825, p. 144.

6.   Unemployment Rates by Occupation and Sex: 1974

(Annual averages)

Major occupation group	Total		Men		Women	
	Black	White	Black	White	Black	White
Total, all civilian workers..............	10.4	5.1	9.7	4.4	11.2	6.2
Experienced labor force	8.7	4.4	8.5	3.9	9.1	5.3
White-collar workers	7.0	3.1	5.5	2.0	7.7	4.2
Professional and technical..................	4.3	2.1	4.3	1.7	4.3	2.8
Managers and administrators,						
except farm	3.3	1.8	3.1	1.5	4.0	3.2
Sales workers..................................	13.9	3.9	12.7	2.8	15.1	5.5
Clerical workers	8.2	4.3	6.7	3.1	8.8	4.6
Blue-collar workers	10.2	6.2	9.3	5.6	13.5	9.0
Craft and kindred workers..................	6.7	4.2	6.5	4.1	(B)	6.1
Operatives, except transport..............	11.8	7.6	10.2	6.3	13.8	9.6
Transport equipment operatives	5.8	4.9	5.9	4.9	(B)	4.8
Nonfarm laborers............................	12.9	9.5	12.7	9.5	(B)	9.0
Service workers.................................	8.7	5.7	9.8	5.2	8.1	6.0
Private household	5.4	3.8	(B)	4.4	5.3	3.7
Other	9.5	5.9	9.6	5.2	9.4	6.4
Farm workers...................................	5.9	2.2	5.6	2.0	(B)	3.1

B   Base less than 75,000.

SOURCE: U.S. Bureau of the Census, *The Social and Economic Status of the Black Population in the United States, 1974*, Current Population Reports, Special Studies, Series P-23, No. 54, p. 69.

7. Unemployment Rates: 1960-1975

■——■ 1960 to 1974—Annual averages
●——● 1974 to 1975—Seasonally adjusted quarterly averages

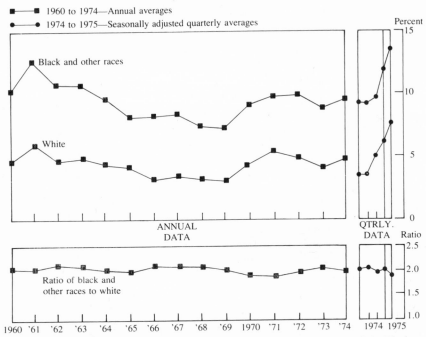

SOURCE: U.S. Bureau of the Census, *The Social and Economic Status of the Black Population in the United States, 1974,* Current Population Reports, Special Studies, Series P-23, No. 54, p. 51.

8.   Computation of NUL Unofficial Unemployment Rate

(Numbers in thousands)

Total	2nd Q. 1974	1st Q. 1975	2nd Q. 1975
Unofficial Unemployed[1]	10,590	15,423	15,267
Official Unemployed	4,608	8,283	8,004
Discouraged Workers[2]	4,745	5,345	5,480
Part-Time Unemployed[3]	1,237	1,795	1,783
Unofficial Civilian Labor Force[1]	95,401	96,497	97,863
Official Civilian Labor Force..............	90,656	91,152	92,383
Discouraged Workers[2]	4,745	5,345	5,480
Unofficial Unemployment Rate	11.1	16.0	15.6
Official Unemployment Rate..............	5.1	9.1	8.7
Blacks[4]			
Unofficial Unemployed.......................	2,232	2,952	3,061
Official Unemployed	935	1,453	1,483
Discouraged Workers	1,067	1,201	1,262
Part-Time Unemployed....................	230	298	314
Unofficial Civilian Labor Force	11,338	11,443	11,708
Official Civilian Labor Force..............	10,271	10,242	10,444
Discouraged Workers	1,067	1,201	1,264
Unofficial Unemployment Rate	19.7	25.8	26.1
Official Unemployment Rate..............	9.1	14.2	14.2
Whites			
Unofficial Unemployed.......................	8,354	12,470	12,206
Official Unemployed	3,672	6,830	6,521
Discouraged Workers	3,676	4,144	4,216
Part-Time Unemployed....................	1,006	1,496	1,469
Unofficial Civilian Labor Force	84,061	85,054	86,155
Official Civilian Labor Force..............	80,385	80,910	81,939
Discouraged Workers	3,676	4,144	4,216
Unofficial Unemployment Rate	9.9	14.7	14.2
Official Unemployment Rate..............	4.6	8.4	8.0

[1]   Numbers are not seasonally adjusted, but are the original, unrevised BLS figures.

[2]   "Discouraged Workers," according to NUL usage, includes *all* persons not in the labor force who "want a job now," while BLS includes only the subgroup who "think they cannot get a job."

[3]   This group constitutes 46 percent of part-time workers who want full-time jobs, according to the U.S. Congress Joint Economic Committee formula.

[4]   Blacks include other non-whites.

SOURCE: National Urban League Research Department, "Quarterly Economic Report on the Black Worker," Second Quarter, 1975, p. 5.

9. Official Unemployment Rates of Black and White
Workers by Sex and Age Status

Percent Unemployed of Total Labor Force[1]			
Type of Workers	2nd Q. 1974	1st Q. 1975	2nd Q. 1975
Total	5.1	9.1	8.7
Black[2]	9.1	14.2	14.2
White	4.6	8.4	8.0
Adult Men			
Black	6.2	12.5	12.0
White	3.1	7.1	6.4
Married Men			
Black	3.8	9.8	9.2
White	2.1	5.7	5.1
Adult Women			
Black	7.3	11.3	11.4
White	4.4	8.0	7.5
Teenage Males			
Black	30.4	38.1	38.0
White	12.6	20.3	18.5
Teenage Females			
Black	34.6	41.3	38.9
White	14.2	17.4	18.0

Number Unemployed in Thousands[1]			
Type of Workers	2nd Q. 1974	1st Q. 1975	2nd Q. 1975
Total	4,608	8,283	8,004
Black[2]	935	1,453	1,483
White	3,672	6,830	6,521
Adult Men			
Black	319	646	621
White	1,385	3,201	2,917
Married Men			
Black	132	338	321
White	779	2,061	1,843
Adult Women			
Black	304	481	489
White	1,211	2,266	2,139
Teenage Males			
Black	164	167	199
White	564	785	816
Teenage Females			
Black	147	157	174
White	511	578	649

[1] Numbers are not seasonally adjusted, but are the original, unrevised BLS figures.

[2] Blacks include other non-whites.

SOURCE: National Urban League Research Department, "Quarterly Economic Report on the Black Worker," Second Quarter, 1975, p. 5.

10.   Median Earnings in 1973 of Civilians 14 Years Old and Over, by Occupation of
Longest Job, Work Experience, and Sex

(Persons as of the following year)

Occupation	Men		Women		Ratio: Black to white	
	Black	White	Black	White	Men	Women
ALL WORKERS						
Total, with earnings..........	$ 5,785	$ 9,046	$3,030	$3,299	0.64	0.92
Professional, technical, and kindred workers..................	9,668	13,142	7,543	6,790	0.74	1.11
Managers and administrators, except farm.......................	9,394	13,831	8,021	5,605	0.68	1.43
Farmers and farm managers......	(B)	5,590	(B)	1,408	(B)	(B)
Clerical and kindred workers.....	8,007	8,905	4,170	4,409	0.90	0.95
Sales workers	4,270	8,952	1,405	1,637	0.48	0.86
Craft and kindred workers	7,346	10,111	4,446	4,357	0.73	1.02
Operatives, including transport workers............................	6,539	7,985	3,629	3,618	0.82	1.00
Private household workers........	(B)	(B)	1,072	364	(B)	2.95
Service workers, except private household	4,562	4,609	2,773	1,663	0.99	1.67
Farm laborers and supervisors...	855	1,384	370	463	0.62	0.80
Laborers, except farm	4,052	3,146	(B)	1,938	1.29	(B)
YEAR-ROUND FULL-TIME WORKERS						
Total, with earnings..........	7,880	11,516	5,487	6,434	0.68	0.85
Professional, technical, and kindred workers..................	10,682	14,455	9,015	9,076	0.74	0.99
Managers and administrators, except farm.......................	11,498	14,662	(B)	7,602	0.78	(B)
Farmers and farm managers......	(B)	6,824	(B)	(B)	(B)	(B)
Clerical and kindred workers.....	9,241	10,811	6,522	6,462	0.85	1.01
Sales workers	(B)	12,415	(B)	4,632	(B)	(B)
Craft and kindred workers	8,857	11,387	(B)	6,224	0.78	(B)
Operatives, including transport workers............................	7,830	9,782	4,824	5,449	0.80	0.89
Private household workers........	(B)	(B)	2,232	1,827	(B)	1.22
Service workers, except private household	6,397	8,618	4,595	4,577	0.74	1.00
Farm laborers and supervisors...	(B)	5,104	(B)	(B)	(B)	(B)
Laborers, except farm	6,554	8,423	(B)	4,722	0.78	(B)

B   Base too small for figure to be shown.

SOURCE: U.S. Bureau of the Census, *The Social and Economic Status of the Black Population in the United States, 1974*, Current Population Reports, Special Studies, Series P-23, No. 54, p. 80.

11. Occupation of Employed Men: 1964, 1970, and 1974

(Annual averages)

Occupation	1964		1970		1974	
	Black and other races	White	Black and other races	White	Black and other races	White
Total employed						
Thousands	4,359	41,114	4,803	44,157	5,179	47,340
Percent	100	100	100	100	100	100
White-collar workers...............	16	41	22	43	24	42
Professional and technical	6	13	8	15	9	15
Medical and other health	1	1	1	1	1	2
Teachers, except college	1	1	1	2	2	2
Other professional and technical workers	4	10	6	12	6	11
Managers and administrators, except farm.....................	3	15	5	15	5	15
Salaried workers	1	9	3	11	4	12
Self-employed workers...	2	6	2	4	2	3
Sales workers	2	6	2	6	2	6
Retail trade	1	2	1	2	1	2
Other industries	1	4	1	4	1	4
Clerical workers..................	5	7	7	7	7	6
Blue-collar workers	58	46	60	46	57	46
Craft and kindred workers.....	12	20	14	21	16	21
Carpenters......................	1	2	1	2	1	2
Construction craft workers, except carpenters	3	4	3	4	4	5
Mechanics and repairers	3	5	5	6	4	6
Metal craft workers	1	3	1	3	1	2
Blue-collar worker supervisors, n.e.c.	2	3	1	3	2	3
All other craft workers	1	4	2	4	3	4
Operatives, except transport..	18	15	21	14	17	12
Transport equipment operatives......................	8	5	7	5	9	6
Nonfarm laborers................	22	6	18	6	15	7
Service workers	16	6	13	6	15	7
Farm workers.......................	10	7	6	5	4	5
Farmers and farm managers...	3	5	2	4	1	3
Farm laborers and supervisors	7	2	4	2	3	2

Note: Beginning with 1971, occupational employment data are not strictly comparable with statistics for 1970 and earlier years as a result of changes in the occupational classification system for the 1970 Census of Population that were introduced in January 1971 and the addition of a question to the Current Population Survey in December 1971 relating to major activities and duties. For an explanation of these changes, see Bureau of the Census, Technical Paper No. 26, and Bureau of Labor Statistics, *Employment and Earnings* (monthly), Explanatory Notes.

SOURCE: U.S. Bureau of the Census, *The Social and Economic Status of the Black Population in the United States, 1974*, Current Population Reports, Special Studies, Series P-23, No. 54, p. 73.

12. Occupation of Employed Women: 1964, 1970, and 1974

(Annual averages)

Occupation	1964		1970		1974	
	Black and other races	White	Black and other races	White	Black and other races	White
Total employed						
Thousands	3,024	20,808	3,642	26,025	4,136	29,280
Percent	100	100	100	100	100	100
White-collar workers...............	22	61	36	64	42	64
Professional and technical.....	8	14	11	15	12	15
Medical and other health	2	4	3	4	4	4
Teachers, except college....	5	6	5	6	5	6
Other professional and technical workers	2	4	3	5	4	5
Managers and administrators, except farm......................	2	5	2	5	2	5
Salaried workers	1	3	1	3	2	4
Self-employed workers......	1	2	1	1	1	1
Sales workers	2	8	3	8	3	7
Retail trade	2	7	2	7	2	6
Other industries	-	1	-	1	-	1
Clerical workers..................	11	34	21	36	25	36
Stenographers, typists, and secretaries..............	4	12	5	13	7	14
Other clerical workers	8	22	16	24	14	17
Blue-collar workers	15	17	19	16	20	15
Craft and kindred workers.....	1	1	1	1	1	2
Operatives, except transport..	14	15	17	14	17	12
Transport equipment operators........................	-	-	-	-	-	1
Nonfarm laborers...............	1	-	1	-	1	1
Service workers	56	19	43	19	37	19
Private household...............	33	5	18	3	11	3
Other...............................	23	14	26	15	26	17
Farm workers........................	6	3	2	2	1	2
Farmers and farm managers......................	1	1	-	-	-	-
Farm laborers and supervisors	5	2	2	2	1	1

Note: Beginning with 1971, occupation employment data are not strictly comparable with statistics for 1970 and earlier years as a result of changes in the occupational classification system for the 1970 Census of Population that were introduced in January 1971 and the addition of a question to the Current Population Survey in December 1971 relating to major activities and duties. For an explanation of these changes, see Bureau of the Census, Technical Paper No. 26, and Bureau of Labor Statistics, *Employment and Earnings* (Monthly), Explanatory Notes.

- Represents zero.

SOURCE: U.S. Bureau of the Census, *The Social and Economic Status of the Black Population in the United States, 1974,* Current Population Reports, Special Studies, Series P-23, No. 54, p. 74.

13. Ratio of White to Negro Workers* by Occupational Field and Sex, 1910-1960

	Male						Female					
	1910	1920	1930	1940	1950	1960	1910	1920	1930	1940	1950	1960
All sectors	1.0	1.0	1.0	1.0	1.0	1.0	1.0	1.0	1.0	1.0	1.0	1.0
Nonfarm, total	1.5	1.4	1.3	1.3	1.1	1.1	1.3	1.6	1.3	1.2	1.1	1.0
White-collar sector, total	6.8	6.6	6.3	3.4	3.8	2.9	12.7	12.7	10.5	7.8	4.5	3.5
Professional & technical	2.9	2.9	2.8	3.2	3.1	3.7	6.6	5.9	4.8	3.4	2.3	2.4
Props., mgrs., & officials	8.1	8.7	7.8	6.4	5.1	6.8	4.9	4.6	4.7	5.7	3.4	2.9
Clerical & sales workers	10.1	8.1	8.3	6.4	3.4	2.0	43.2	34.2	30.5	21.3	6.9	4.7
Manual & service sector, total	1.1	1.0	0.9	0.9	0.8	0.7	1.0	0.8	0.6	0.6	0.5	0.5
Skilled workers & foremen	4.3	4.0	3.7	3.6	2.4	2.1	30.5	13.9	12.1	7.1	2.5	1.6
Operatives & semiskilled	2.5	2.0	1.7	1.5	1.0	0.8	5.2	3.5	2.6	2.1	1.3	1.0
Laborers	0.7	0.5	0.5	0.4	0.3	0.3	1.5	0.9	0.8	1.1	0.5	1.4
Service workers	0.2	0.2	0.2	0.4	0.4	0.4	0.4	0.3	0.3	0.3	0.3	0.3
Farm, total	0.6	0.6	0.6	0.5	0.6	0.6	0.2	0.2	0.2	0.1	0.3	0.4

* Relative to their number in total work force.

SOURCE: Eli Ginzberg and Dale L. Hiestand, "Employment Patterns of Negro Men and Women," in *The American Negro Reference Book,* edited by John P. Davis (Englewood Cliffs, N.J.: Prentice-Hall, 1966), p. 233.

14. Percent Distribution of White and Negro Employed by Occupational Fields, 1910-1960

	1910		1920		1930		1940		1950		1960	
	White	Negro	White	Negro	White	Negro	White	Negro	White	Negro	White	Negro
All sectors	100.0	100.0	100.0	100.0	100.0	100.0	100.0*	100.0*	100.0*	100.0*	100.0*	100.0*
Nonfarm, total	72.0	49.6	76.0	53.4	80.6	63.9	82.3	66.6	81.6	79.5	89.6	83.6
White-collar sector, total	23.8	3.0	27.8	3.6	33.0	4.6	35.7	6.0	39.9	10.2	44.1	13.4
Professional & tech.	4.8	1.4	5.3	1.5	6.5	2.1	8.0	2.7	8.6	3.4	11.9	4.7
Props., mgrs. & offcls.	7.4	0.8	7.4	0.8	8.3	1.0	9.0	1.3	9.8	2.0	9.1	1.4
Clerical & Sales	11.6	0.8	15.1	1.3	18.2	1.5	18.7	2.0	21.5	4.8	23.1	7.3
Manual & service sector	48.2	46.6	48.2	49.8	47.6	59.3	46.6	60.6	47.7	69.3	45.5	70.3
Skilled	13.0	2.5	14.5	3.0	14.2	3.2	12.2	3.0	14.4	5.5	14.3	6.1
Semiskilled & operative	16.1	5.4	16.8	7.3	17.2	9.4	19.0	10.3	20.3	18.3	18.3	19.6
Laborers	14.3	17.4	13.4	20.8	11.7	21.6	6.1	14.3	5.0	15.7	4.0	12.6
Service	4.8	21.3	3.5	18.7	4.5	25.1	9.3	33.0	8.0	29.8	8.9	31.9
Farm, total	28.0	50.4	24.1	46.6	19.4	36.1	16.7	32.8	11.1	19.0	5.9	8.1

* Sum of items does not equal 100.0 because of those for whom no occupation was reported.

SOURCE: Eli Ginzberg and Dale L. Hiestand, "Employment Patterns of Negro Men and Women," in *The American Negro Reference Book*, edited by John P. Davis (Englewood Cliffs, N.J.: Prentice-Hall, 1966), p. 220.